THE
FANGIRL
LIFE

THE FANGIRL LIFE

A GUIDE TO FEELING
ALL THE FEELS
AND LEARNING
HOW TO DEAL

Kathleen Smith

A TarcherPerigee Book

tarcherperigee

An imprint of Penguin Random House LLC
375 Hudson Street, New York, New York 10014

Illustrations by Camilla Fiocchi. Copyright © 2016 by Kathleen Smith

LIBRARY OF CONGRESS CATALOGING-IN-PUBLICATION DATA

Names: Smith, Kathleen, 1985– author.
Title: The fangirl life : a guide to feeling all the feels and learning how to deal / Kathleen Smith.
Description: First edition. | New York, New York : Perigee, 2016.
Identifiers: LCCN 2015041656 | ISBN 9781101983690
Subjects: LCSH: Young women—Social life and customs. | Young women—Psychology. | Fans (Persons)—Psychology. | Identity (Psychology) | Mass Media and culture. | Subculture.
Classification: LCC HQ798.S5695 2016 | DDC 305.242/2—dc23

First edition: July 2016

PRINTED IN THE UNITED STATES OF AMERICA

1   3   5   7   9   10   8   6   4   2

Text design by Sabrina Bowers
Set in Wile Roman Pro

Most Perigee books are available at special quantity discounts for bulk purchases for sales promotions, premiums, fund-raising, or educational use. Special books, or book excerpts, can also be created to fit specific needs. For details, write: SpecialMarkets@penguinrandomhouse.com.

For my parents,
who welcomed television into our home like an old friend.

CONTENTS

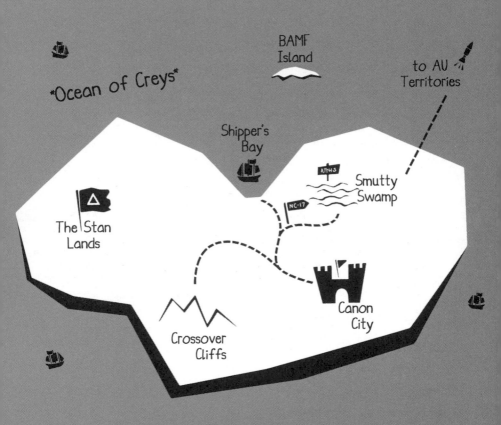

INTRODUCTION

I watch television like it's a spectator sport. I laugh, I scream, I cry. I even jump up and down. Then I get on the computer and do it all over again with a group of people who totally get it.

—JANA, TWENTY-FOUR

There are only two things I love in this world: everybody and television.

—KENNETH PARCELL, *30 ROCK*

The best day of my life was the day I stood on the top step of the Lincoln Memorial wearing nothing but stuffed animals. Depreciated Beanie Babies, squeaky chew toys, and fuzzy baby rattlers cascaded down to my knees in a dress secured by my father's finest fishing line. *Abe Schmabe,* I thought as I grinned like an idiot and posed with another Japanese tourist from the line that had begun to form. An elderly woman poked at a mooing cow on my dress, not comprehending that my ensemble was an ode to the Lady Gaga costume made by Rachel Berry on *Glee,* but I didn't mind, because I had *arrived.*

Every star will tell you there was a moment when he or she knew that they had made it. Perhaps my moment should have been the day I got accepted to Harvard or the day I sat across the room from my first therapy client. But I was twenty-five years old, and I had just given up wearing pants for a year because of a fictional character. And on that lovely October day in the most powerful city in the world, I hot glued a unicorn to a headband and let the world see for the first time what I really was: a fangirl.

What exactly is a fangirl? If you're waiting for a sloppy urban dictionary quote, you won't find it here. A fangirl is simply a lady fan. If you want to get technical, the nineteenth-century origin of the word *fan* is somewhat disputed. It's either an abbreviation of the word *fancy* (British-speak for enjoying something a lot) or the word *fanatic* (a state that is about twenty light-years past liking something). This uncertain etymology lesson brilliantly sums up the quixotic nature of the fangirl brain. How does thinking, "Hey, this episode of *Supernatural* is really cool!" turn into iron-pressing Jared Padalecki's face onto your pillowcase? Or in my personal history, how did admiring a *Glee* character's wardrobe lead to hanging half of it in my closet?

Fangirls also come in all shapes and sizes, so people shouldn't expect to be able to pick us out of a lineup if all our Threadless shirts are in the dirty laundry pile—even you, a fangirl yourself, won't immediately recognize your kind by sight alone. We are old and young and in the middle. We're straight, gay, bisexual, and everything else under the rainbow. Remember the girl sitting behind you in math class who asked you what day it was? (Shhh, it's October third!) She wrote the forty-thousand-word *Sherlock* fic you have bookmarked on your smartphone. Your crabby boss has been working on her Comic Con costume all weekend. Your computer science professor got her start by teaching herself HTML for her *X-Files* fanpage. Appearances can be deceiving, as we have a tendency to hide distinctive facets of our personality when faced with stigmatization. Who hasn't leaked a strangled yelp of embarrassment when a family member sees fan fiction reviews on her email account? Perhaps you've called into work sick after a series finale, knowing that the world is not prepared for the emotional crisis your feels hath unleashed. Or maybe you've even scared away potential mates on a first date when asked about your passions.

I have been a fangirl for as long as I can remember. In kindergarten I sneaked dog-eared *Playbills* under my pajamas for my nightly bath, where I'd flip through the soggy pages and gaze longingly at the actresses. My Barbie doll escapades were fraught with comedic storylines. When *Star Wars* was rereleased, my parents hunkered down, waiting for the incessant banging of John Williams's "Han Solo and the Princess" on our ancient piano to stop. Rinse and repeat. There have been many moments in my life when I thought I would never again love a story as fiercely as I did right then. But some powerhouse female or truly marvelous plot always came along and rewoke the beast.

My passion for fiction landed me in a career that helps people work through their own life sagas. As a licensed therapist, I've dedicated a lot of energy and thought to understanding how a fangirl ticks and what exactly makes her unique. Are we products of our environment or our genetic makeup? Have millions of years of evolution made us vulnerable to the angsty glances exchanged over our favorite ship, or is seeing subtext a sixth sense, a sort of fangirl superpower, like X-ray vision? I believe that the more we are able to appreciate our unique talents, the more we can advocate for fangirl acceptance in the mainstream. For we have suffered too long among people whose supposed deficiency in social functioning has historically justified their persecution. Like English majors. Or gingers.

If you look closely, you'll find that the time is ripe for us to take a few bold steps. Emerging technology and social media play a huge role in creating the conditions that sprout fangirls. We've multiplied faster than our own plot bunnies, and there is no effective hater-based contraception to stop us. Forty years ago, a fangirl pissed off by a character death would have to take the trouble to actually write a letter, address and stamp an envelope, and mail it to vent. Today, we have 140 characters at our fingertips and the whole world as our audience. We are able to reach across the globe to build communities in fandoms. We carve out little fiefdoms with the common love of a middle-aged actress, and we march up the gangplank to board our favorite crackship. A million friendships blossom over the prospect of two fictional people finally doing the deed. In short, it's a beautiful time to be a fangirl.

Fangirls are also charged with the task of overcoming stereotypes. Perhaps sometimes you feel crushed by the weight of the typecasting that pervades social media and beyond. You're not the girl who turns into a howler monkey when an actor favorites a tweet or the woman who gets arrested at cons for attacking her favorite Marvel superhero. Fangirling is a spectrum, and those who settle into a comfortable spot somewhere between passive television watching and full-blown psychosis aren't sure whether they should fade into the wallpaper or stand up to be counted. The world was never quite ready for you, but here you are. So what are you going to do about it?

This is the part where I'm supposed to say, "Live. Live, you beautiful unicorn!" But it's not that simple. As a therapist, I help others grapple with issues of identity. To cope with the anxiety that emerges when you try to honor your values and your imagination. But then I slink home and silently squee over a spoiler or the latest update to a novel-length fanfic. Writing about the fangirl world began as an adventure for me, testing the idea that both of these parts of myself are congruous. Because I believe there is a connection between finding the motivation for success and unleashing the unabashed joy of what I can create in my busy little head. This book is my best attempt to hammer a few solid planks between these two worlds, with enough space for you to take a big, brave leap from where I leave you.

In my tiny corner of the fangirl universe, I have tried my

best to construct a theory for self-improvement that simultaneously honors our way of life. The lens I use to understand the psychology of the experience draws heavily from my own theoretical orientation as a therapist, with a few pinches of creys and creativity added here and there. This lens operates under the assumption that swimming in anxiety every day is not an enjoyable experience, and that we would all be better off if we could poke our heads above the water more often than not.

My second assumption is that we could all benefit from adopting some of the traits we admire in fictional characters. Not the illegal or scientifically daunting ones, obviously, but the traits that shine in common across fictional worlds and genres and draw our finger to the page or the screen as we whisper to ourselves, "Why can't I be like that?" So in short, Less Anxiety, More Awesome. I think that's a slogan most of us can get behind.

Is This Book for Me?

If you really enjoy something, and you identify as a lady, then congratulations! You're in the club. I like to keep the definition broad, because the fangirl historically has been pigeonholed into any number of tropes. But with the rise of the Internet, generally anyone who enjoys a TV show or a celebrity can be rewarded with the ability to learn more about that interest and connect with others who share it.

Fandom is deep and wide, but there's a reason this book

Introduction

isn't titled *The Fanperson Life*. Fan culture examined by the field of psychology is an unending parade of men addressing men. Fanboys get their share of attention, from Comic Con panels to books on using Batman in the counseling room. There are also countless thoughtful critiques about the presence of misogyny in fan culture. But boys, you've had your time in the sun, and this one's for the ladies. There are tribes within fan culture, but the fangirl is always typecast as the fourteen-year-old sobbing endlessly at a Bieber concert or the lone lady in a *Dungeons and Dragons* game. Many would be surprised to find that there is a whole world of women and girls who dedicate a significant portion of their energy and emotions into the concept of story found in countless genres. These women are often left out when you limit your definition of fangirl to geek or music culture.

This book is a tribute to my fiction-loving tribe. It's for the law student who unearths strength from the strut of a TV attorney. For the mother who unwinds with a glass of wine and a little bit of zombie apocalypse. For the teenager who points to a novel's heroine and says, "Yes. I'll have more of that please." To the women and girls who get that forming online friendships isn't a symptom of isolation from reality but an opportunity to form common bonds that will cheer us through our victories and comfort us when life gets rough. So if you're not sure whether you belong to our fangirl tribe, I've provided a few examples to evaluate yourself. If you don't know whether a friend or family member is a fangirl, then please put the book down for a second and ask her. She'll probably be happy to talk about it to someone other than her secret Twitter account's followers.

You Might Be a Fangirl If . . .

- You survive boring meetings by imagining two fictional characters making out in a variety of settings.

- You have assumed the fetal position on the floor during an emotional scene.

- You have posted a lengthy diatribe on the Internet defending a fictional character's choice.

- When someone asks what your favorite season is, you automatically answer with a season of a TV show instead of, say, summer or fall.

- You live-tweet yourself watching a friend watch a show you love.

- You frequently get carsick from reading fan fiction on your smartphone.

- Netflix has presented you with the "Are you still watching?" button at least once.

- You were disappointed when the TV show *Shipping Wars* was entirely different from what you had anticipated.

- You can identify the current story arc of a show based on a female character's hair.

You can 100 percent still be a fangirl if none of these extremes applies to you. Just because you don't spend your time illegally downloading the Lifetime movies in which your favorite celebrity had a three-word role doesn't mean you aren't allowed to appreciate her. The fangirl way of life doesn't belong in a box any more than my "I Met Li'l Sebastian at the Pawnee Harvest Festival" T-shirt belongs at the bottom of my closet. Wear it proudly, and don't let anyone tell you what you are or aren't.

If you aren't bold enough to define yourself to others, the world will smack a label on you faster than Ryan Murphy can ruin your life with a television show. There are about a zillion myths about fangirls floating around these days. Many of these false assumptions sting those dipping their toes into the wading pool of fandom. So before you decide to avoid the label of fangirl altogether, you should be aware of the myths that spew from the mouths of haters.

MYTH 1: FANGIRLS ARE ALL TEENAGERS. The first fangirl friend I ever met in real life was a wonderfully intelligent and successful woman in her forties. Sure there are herds of thirteen-year-olds lurking about the Web crying about not having enough allowance money for concert tickets, but many of us are college age and beyond. Is it more socially acceptable for a teenager to cry about Sirius Black than your grandmother? Yes. But that doesn't mean the middle-aged ladies of the world aren't secretly pining over Julianna Margulies's eyebrows or Claire Underwood's wardrobe in their free time.

MYTH 2: FANGIRLS ARE TRYING TO ESCAPE THEIR BORING LIVES.

False. Why do people paint fangirls as Lady Ediths left at home to mope? We have hobbies that don't involve making gifs or crying. We go on adventures with friends and family. We have killer careers. Some of us even care about sportsball! Fangirls can have rich lives just like other people. The difference is that we just have six thousand imaginary friends along for the ride. Also, we might not feel the need to share too much about non-feels-related endeavors on the Internet.

MYTH 3: FANGIRLS AREN'T CAPABLE OF HEALTHY RELATIONSHIPS.

What is it about the Internet that makes people think all of our fangirl friends are serial killers or proselytizing lesbians preying on straight girls? All of a sudden we're all *Orange Is the New Black* characters. Engaging in fandom and participating in healthy family, friend, and romantic relationships aren't mutually exclusive. Anything can become unhealthy if you focus on it too intensely, real-world relationships and online relationships alike.

MYTH 4: FANGIRLS SPEND ALL DAY ON THE INTERNET.

Fine, this is 100 percent true. I'm on the Internet right now, scrolling past cat gifs. Haters gonna hate. Fangirls have been known, from time to time, to hang up our clicky fingers and breathe some fresh air and go hiking and stuff. How else do you think we come up with vacation headcanon for our OTP?

The Power of Story

There are some people in this world who can sample a tiny spoonful of gelato and walk out the door with their money still in their pockets. And then there are some of us who proceed to buy the entire country of Italy. It's often an all or nothing world for the fangirl who has yet to learn to bridle the imagination. She is notorious for being incapable of passively enjoying stories. She takes them and makes them hers with that special stamp of inspiration.

For years I have studied and written about the art of psychotherapy, a profession whose efforts could be summed up with one simple question—what motivates people? Psychologists spend a great deal of energy debating this very question, and for years I piled theory after theory into my tired grad student head without bothering to ask myself, "What motivates me?" When I finally did just that, my brain rolled out the confetti cannons.

I know this much is true: Story motivates me. Story is powerful, and it doesn't matter whether it's coming from across the table or from my Netflix account. All too often I fail to remember in my own life that the bad weeks are part of a larger story. A story where I am my author, my protagonist, and my audience. Life is a lot like television when you think about it. Sometimes days can seem as uneventful as a midseason hiatus. Or times get tricky as new characters emerge, people we loathe as much as the nastiest villain on *American Horror Story*. But the beautiful thing about reality is that unlike TV, we can start a new season of life whenever we feel like it.

We also have neuroscience on our side. Brain images have only recently begun to reveal what fangirls have known to be true all along—that story is a powerful stimulant with tremendous influence over how we think and act. Like meth, only safer. Research also tells us that fiction cognitively and emotionally transports us into the minds of our favorite characters, making the average fanfic writer more equipped for empathy and interpersonal interaction than her nonfiction reading peers. So *boom!* Tell that to your mom.

Choosing to see my own life as a narrative has been the handiest choice I have ever made. I started examining the characters who were mileposts in my fangirl journey, the Leia Organas, and the Laura Roslins, and the Leslie Knopes of fiction. And I began to realize that my favorite characters weren't the ones who entered the story in total control of their lives and emotions. I rooted for the people who all too often fell short. I treasured the characters who made bad decisions. I chose the underdogs who heard *no* more often than they heard *yes.* So why was I so afraid to start cheering for myself the same way?

As a fangirl, you have inspiration at your fingertips every time a screen blinks to life or a page is turned. You have community by your side when you have made a Walter White–level bad decision. Your imagination is there to amaze and entertain you when the rest of the world is slingshotting wingless birds across their smartphone screens. You are more equipped for a fabulous life than you ever realized, but sometimes you choose to hide behind your passions rather than be fueled by them. There is absolutely nothing wrong with being unusual because it's the currency that keeps the world turning and worth writing about.

In the coming chapters, I'll examine the ups and downs of the fangirl life. Because not every moment is as carefree or as plot-worthy as you'd like. Stirring up all that tasty emotion over a celebrity or a novel on a regular basis can make you anxious. You lose focus at school or work until you can hide yourself in a bathroom stall to properly freak out over the latest spoilers. Maybe you encounter other fans who are downright spiteful and turn the whole experience into a popularity contest. Sometimes you may find that you've lost the graciousness of your friends and family when you can't give them your full attention. Maybe you find yourself playing it safe, propagating someone else's intellectual property because you're too scared to create your own worlds. Or perhaps worst of all, you realize that you spend too much time agonizing over the imaginary when real-life opportunities are snapping their fingers in front of your face.

In this book I want to be able to shine a light on the good of fangirling but also provide some constructive advice and reflection on how to handle the not so good. Because I do believe balance is possible and probable if you can engage your imagination and direct it toward your day-to-day life. There you will find that you can make your own world and star in it. Where the perfect lines are the ones coming out of your mouth and not a movie star's, and badassery is yours for the taking. Where you aren't guided by people's perceptions or the need for acceptance or attention, but by the narrative you want your life to tell. I know what you're thinking: Lofty goals, much? But why not? If our heads are already in the stars, we might as well shoot for them. I choose to trust that there is a way to stand up and be counted as both a fangirl and a woman worthy of deepest respect. To live a story as transformative as the ones to which we dedicate our imaginations.

How to Read the Book

With your eyes! Kidding. As a scholar of many fandoms, I have tried to incorporate the breadth of the fangirl world into the text. The book is a veritable *Gilmore Girls* episode of pop culture references, so don't feel bad if you don't catch every 1990s sitcom or space opera reference. Google it. Don't Google it. Tweet me and ask me to rant less about Shonda Rhimes and help you with your 5 Seconds of Summer obsession instead. Cross out a gross ship name and add your own. Make this book yours, and don't be afraid to doodle in it.

Each chapter breaks down what I view to be the basics of fangirling. I'll examine the good, the bad, and the hairporn, while also providing you with some real-life science and some helpful exercises for applying the principles to your life. I'll teach you how to diagnose common fangirl disorders and treat them. I will talk about fan fiction, shipping, and how to move forward when a character dies. Finally, we'll examine what it means to transform from fangirl into the fanwoman you would like to be. If you want to read straight through without stopping, I would encourage you to go back and try out some of the exercises at the end of each chapter. These activities will help you glean real-world inspiration from your fictional favorites. Also, feel free to flip to the back of the book, where you'll find a few fun nuggets.

If you enjoy squeeflailing over a pretty fictional lady or speculating endlessly over plot points, but you would like to carve more space for the narrative of your own life, then I think that this book has something to offer you. Thanks to many of my gracious friends, online and offline, I will pull from more than my own experiences. Although I did watch a crap ton of Netflix to prep for this book. You're welcome.

So let's get started. Don't worry; your OTP's fanfic page will still be there when you get back!

CHAPTER 1
THE FANGIRL BRAIN

> I totally had a nightmare starring Twisty the Clown last night, but I escaped him because I am the Lana Winters of my own dream sequences.
>
> —JESS, TWENTY-FOUR

> This is my hard drive and it only makes sense to put things in there that are useful. Really useful. Ordinary people fill their heads with all kinds of rubbish.
>
> —SHERLOCK

The fangirl brain is a brilliant space, or as Sherlock might say, a mind palace. Somehow we manage to make room in our minds for empathy, intellectual pursuit, and speculation about whether two fictional idiots will ever kiss. But addiction, anxiety, and self-doubt also carve out their territories. They are monsters that romp north of The Wall and threaten to spill over into the more civilized parts of you.

In this chapter, I'll give you a tour of your brain, exploring both the beautiful and the not so beautiful. On our trip, I'll break down three functions of the brain that prevent you from reaching your fangirl potential: addiction, habit, and self-doubt. I'll explain the science of getting hooked on a TV show, and we'll examine the not-so-great routines of fangirling. Then you'll enroll in Defense Against the Dark Voices 101, where we'll talk about the enemy inside our minds. Finally, we'll examine how ready you are to make big changes in your life as you move through the book.

The Roller Coaster of Addiction

Fangirls get addicted to stuff. Super shocking! We're all too eager to hop on the ride, but then suddenly we can't find the exit sign. When I was first learning about the science of addiction in graduate school, it surprised me to learn that people develop a dependency on a substance or a behavior because they physiologically *crave* stress. The thing about stress is that you always assume that it's bad news, but your life would be dull without it. You wouldn't enter a haunted house or watch *Vampire Diaries* if you didn't crave stress. It keeps your brain alert, and when you're alert, you're likely to do everything just a little bit better. The fangirl brain is no different, always searching for that perfect, plot-twisting story that keeps your eyes wide open and your arms flapping.

The problem is that when you skydive into feels too much, you forget what it feels like to have some good solid ground beneath you. The desire to replicate the jump over and over can lead to obsession or addiction. A giant splat. Fortunately for us, scientists actually know a lot about addiction and how it looks in the brain. Though addictions like drug or alcohol abuse obviously produce more serious impairment to the brain than your seventeenth rewatch of *Veronica Mars*, the neurological processes look similar in several ways. If you don't believe me, let's do a dopamine test!

YEAH, SCIENCE! Turn off the TV. Tell your cat to shut up because you're doing science. Sit up straight with your feet on the floor. Close your eyes and think about a fangirl moment where you were puking rainbows: a first kiss between characters, your first real-life glance of a celebrity, or a spoiler that blew your mind. Got it? Now latch on to that image like you're trying to use it to fly to Neverland, but keep your feet on the ground. Can you feel the buzz of that unicorn vibe? That's dopamine at work. Dopamine is a feel-good chemical, and your brain wants as much of it as it can get.

What's funny about dopamine is that more often than not, that highest high occurs right before a big moment. Maybe you're hiding your little head in your sweatshirt because your ship is about to bang, or perhaps you're Gene Kelly-ing around a lamppost because Twitter told you your fave was cast in a new pilot. In our brains, the largest explosions of dopamine occur *before* the reward. This anticipation causes your body to pump oxygen and glucose even faster to your brain, which is why you often feel as high as a kite the day an Avengers movie is released

#FanficPizza

#FanartPuppy

DOPAMINE

or the minute you're humming the *Doctor Who* opening theme song. In turn, these feels fuel us to keep reading, keep watching, or keep pawing at a screencap making sad llama noises. Completely harmless, right?

RUNNING ON EMPTY. So here's the problem. When some people finish a great movie or series, their dopamine levels drop back to normal. But when a fangirl reads the last sentence of *Harry Potter and the Deathly Hallows*, her brain struggles to keep track of the dopamine reserves, and they dip just a tiny bit below normal. (Like when you think you have enough cell phone data to survive a weekend at your wireless grandma's house, but then you totally don't because your friend texted you that YouTube video of a cat that thinks it's a horse.) So when your dopamine reserves dip below normal, you experience sadness or irritability. You get all Internet ragey or crawl under your covers and never leave.

Wanting to avoid icky emotions, you might begin to seek out an even greater level of stimulus to achieve the soaring heights of crey. If you bombard your dopamine receptors, they have to compensate by becoming less sensitive to the addiction. It takes more and more to achieve the same effect, and if we can't get there, woe unto us. This is called habituation (why I could eventually go from watching three *Breaking Bad* episodes in a row to watching six). So all of a sudden, we don't *want* to check our phones. We HAVE to. We NEED to. Our very lives depend on it, and they become consumed by it. And this, my friends, is what we call addiction.

There's Nothing Wrong with Me!

Science is great, but how do you actually know when you cross the line from fan to fanatic? What counts as obsession and what counts as having a healthy respect for Tina Fey stripping down to her Spanx on *The Late Show*? The unfair truth is that some people are more likely to develop an obsession than others. Your past experiences and environments, and even your time in the womb, influence your susceptibility to hairporn. But the immediate anxieties of day-to-day life also play a role. Scientists have found that if you stress out a rat before you give him a giant bowl of cocaine, guess what? He wants seconds. Short-term stressors create increases in dopamine, and then the fangirl brain releases them in huge amounts. It doesn't know how to ration the goods.

If you're wondering whether you're like that coke-sniffing rat, I've created a Fangirl Obsession Questionnaire for you. In the FOQ, the term *fangirl interest* could refer to a TV show, book, series, band, or actor—basically whatever you're evaluating as an obsession. Also, remember that this is not a tested psychological questionnaire. Go see a professional for one of those. This questionnaire can help you think about the impact of your intense feels and how to generate that motivation to extract your butt from the couch or take a break from the computer screen. So take a look!

Fangirl Obsession Questionnaire

ANSWER THE QUESTIONS BELOW WITH *YAS* OR *NOPE.*

1. Do you experience urges to watch, read, or listen to your fangirl interest?

2. Do you engage with fandom for longer periods of time or more closely than you intended?

3. Do you want to cut down on your fangirling but struggle to do so?

4. Do you spend a lot of time, energy, and/or money in relation to fangirling?

5. Do you fall behind at work, school, or home responsibilities because of your fangirl interest?

6. Do you continue to engage with fangirling, even when it causes problems in relationships?

7. Do you forsake socializing because of fangirling?

8. Do you find yourself needing more and more input from your interest to achieve the same level of engagement as in the past?

9. Do you experience symptoms of withdrawal when you are not fangirling?

10. Do you continue to engage with your interest even when it causes anxiety, stress, or other emotional problems?

If you answered yas to two or three of the questions, you might have a mild obsession. Four to five yases indicate a moderate obsession. Six or more yases indicate that you may need to cut back on the squeeflailing and seek additional tactics for reducing stress and changing habits. Let's take a look at some fangirl-tailored strategies right now.

Changing Your Habits

If addiction is the roller coaster in your brain, then habits are the gears that keep the ride going. Just like that acne-ridden fifteen-year-old smashing the start button at Six Flags, your brain is largely run on autopilot. Maybe you don't feel like you've quite reached the level of addiction I've just described, but you're wondering how on earth to change some of those tricky habits you just can't seem to break. It may take twenty-one days to form a habit, but it takes twenty-one seconds for you to find yourself in a fangirl situation. So the odds can feel stacked against you when you're struggling to be healthy.

When I asked my friends what their worst fangirl habits were, here's what they said.

- Watching TV instead of doing my work

- Daydreaming about my OTP when I'm out with friends

- Excusing myself early from social situations to get back online

- Checking Tumblr tags I know damn well have no new content

- Letting post-TV hangovers affect my work the next day

We've all been there at one point or another. Good and bad, habits form because every human brain is built to conserve energy. If you repeat a behavior long enough, like taking a shower, driving to work, or checking Instagram, then that action will eventually shift to autopilot. Wherever we choose to place our attention, our behaviors tag along behind us. The problem is that turning off the autopilot can be quite difficult. If you don't believe me, think about how many times you check social media every day without even thinking about it. The average person unlocks her phone 110 times a day. Unless Beyoncé is dropping 110 albums every day, then this is completely unnecessary.

Fictional characters don't seem to have as much trouble with bad habits or making significant changes. We see transformation happen over and over again in our favorite stories, and then beat ourselves up when we can't do the same. A villain is confronted with the error of his ways, and he starts leading a better life. An addict hits rock bottom and has nowhere to go but up. Your favorite lady realizes she's been shutting people out her entire life and finally reaches for love. Everything about fiction tells us that change is romantic, sudden, and powerful. But the reality couldn't be further from the truth. You might try the fangirl tricks, like reading an inspirational quote or staring at a motivational pic of a badass character. But it's never quite enough to really change a behavior you want to kick.

Real-life change doesn't make a good screenplay because change is slow, incremental, and a struggle. It can't be condensed into a thirty-second montage with an angry Kelly Clarkson song. We live in a world where "5 Easy Steps!" is the most popular headline used for self-help articles, but the truth is, change can be mother-effing hard. But that doesn't mean it's not worth it. Learning new behaviors takes practice, just like writing really good smutfic takes time, patience, and poor vocabulary choices along the way (Buttcheeks? Really?). So if you want to start living a different kind of life, here's a formula you can follow. Fortunately for you, the fangirl already has most of these skills at her disposal.

STEP 1. REROUTE YOUR NEURONS. Chances are you already talk to yourself anyway, so begin by starting an inner monologue about the change you want to make. Tell yourself what's going to happen. For example, "I'm going to turn my laptop off at 10 P.M. even if I don't feel like it." Then start writing it down. Write it down in a journal. Write it on a piece of paper and stick it in your sock drawer. Type it on a screencap of Lana Parrilla and save it on your desktop. Say it out loud again. Say it front of the mirror. Write a letter to yourself. (Who doesn't love mail?) But shhhhh, don't tell anyone! Science tells us that we're more likely to accomplish goals when we don't tell them to other people. This is because yakking about our intentions boosts our self-esteem enough that we don't feel like we have to do anything else. So keep your plans a secret for now.

STEP 2. ACTIVATE HEADCANON. You're already good about weaving little bits of story for fictional people, right? So activate that headcanon and write an epic tale in your brain

about how you're actually going to pull this off. Perhaps you're the young ingénue with secret ninja skills who's going to run her first 10K. When you construct the story, you also have to be realistic about all the crap that's going to stand in your way and how you're going to take it down like a Dalek. So maybe as the tension rises in your headcanon, there will be antagonists who try to persuade you to watch *Real Housewives* reruns instead of hitting the treadmill. Next, think about how wonderful it will feel when you've accomplished your goal. You're crossing the finish line as a Florence + the Machine song blasts over the speakers. Your hair still looks surprisingly on point. You're jumping into the arms of some random hottie. Being able to visualize yourself bobbing and weaving around the temptations of life is powerful, so don't be surprised if you find this headcanon tugging you toward a new routine.

STEP 3. **STAGE A DRESS REHEARSAL.** Now it's time to start putting yourself in situations (safe ones!) where you need to enact your new behaviors. Pay attention to your anxiety or negative thoughts as you start to act boldly. You might not succeed at first, but keep practicing, and keep repeating steps 1 and 2. I suggest you pick a smallish change to start, like not checking social media compulsively or making your bed every day. If this seems like a lot of work, that's because it is. This is what we call nonfiction. Above all, be kind to your mind! If it helps, think of your brain as the *Millennium Falcon*. It requires a lot of tinkering and a few false starts to really get moving, but when it does, holy crap does it fly.

Where Do I Even Start?

Before you throw the TV off the roof in defeat, let me assure you that fangirling isn't necessarily a negative way for your brain to respond to stress or anxiety. It's unhealthy only when you think it's the only way to get baptized into dopamine heaven. The most successful humans have multiple strategies for dealing with stress in their lives. They exercise or practice mindfulness or lean on good friends in addition to wading through the Internet. So rather than cutting off the feels cold turkey, you can reprogram your brain by starting with small but significant changes. This book is packed with exercises that promote healthy habits and help you steer clear of addiction. But let's start by building some momentum with tiny changes you can make this very second.

EAVESDROP ON YOUR BODY. You should pay as close attention to your body as you do to a cast interview at Paley-Fest. In other words, *be all over it.* Trouble with sleep, lack of energy, muscle tension, and eating changes are all indicators that something might be wrong. My body is telling me right now that I should not have eaten that cookie dough in the bathtub. Connect how you feel with what you've been doing, and consider keeping a chart to track your energy level throughout the week. Correlation is not always causation, but if you feel achy and tired in the morning because you stayed up until 2 A.M. reading Steve and Bucky fanfic, then there's your culprit.

CALL FOR REINFORCEMENTS. You don't hesitate for a second to cry out for help when you need a download link or confirmation of a spoiler. So why the hesitation when your mental and physical health are at stake? If you feel like your obsessions are keeping you from the life you want, then talk to your friends about it. See how you can encourage each other. It also never hurts to make an appointment with your doctor or a mental health professional. Something doesn't have to be wrong with you for you to benefit from solid consultation about your health. Never assume that they won't understand your unicorn self! My clients never knew they were consulting with someone who'd written *Glee* fanfic. If a professional doesn't know what fangirling is, then tell her. By helping her understand, you're also helping other fangirls in the future.

ACTIVATE THE BIG THREE. No, SuperWhoLockians, not everything is about you. Water, exercise, and sunlight are three natural antidepressants that everyone needs. So if you're not sure where to start with reducing stress and developing good habits, this is a no-brainer. You should be hydrating like a goddess and moving your body every day. And while you might hiss at the sunlight on your first trip out of your fangirl cave, eventually you'll grow to love the outdoors.

Defense against the Dark Voices

So this is the point in the story where I have to introduce you to our villain. Because every good plot needs a greasy-haired scoundrel to root against. So let's expand on our metaphor: if addiction is the roller-coaster ride in our brain, and habits keep the gears turning, then there must be someone who keeps us from getting off the ride and getting the nachos we deserve. And this monster is what we call self-doubt.

I have become so acquainted with my self-doubt over the years that I decided to give this negative voice a name. So I named him Carl. You see, Carl is always quick to share his opinion with me about how things are going in my life. Carl thinks this is the dumbest book. Carl tells me I should be working harder, getting up earlier, and eating fewer carbs. Carl whispers in my ear that I have no clue what I'm doing in most areas of my life, and that I should probably give up now and dedicate my life to watching *Frasier* reruns. If Carl sounds like an asshole, well then that's because he is. That is [insert Chris Traeger voice] *literally* his job.

Like any human, sometimes I struggle with negative thinking. Turning off self-doubt is about as easy as turning off gravity. Even when you know you're being irrational, it can seem impossible to do anything different. Giving your self-doubt a name is a technique used in a type of counseling called narrative therapy. When you give a problem a name, you are "externalizing" it. You must externalize to understand that you were never the problem. The problem is the problem. If I'm thinking that I'm going to fail at a task, like never finish this book, then that seems pretty daunting. But if Carl says I am, well then what does he know? Suddenly I'm energized to take risks and prove this jerkface wrong. Carl's opinion means about as much to me as an Internet troll or a plotline from the twenty-ninth season of *Grey's Anatomy*.

If you want to give this technique a try, pick a name for your self-doubt. Maybe visualize a villain from fiction whom you despise and can associate with the name. Please don't pick that glorious yet emotionally repressed female tyrant whom you'll starting shipping with everybody. Pick someone you really can't stand. Like Joffrey from *Game of Thrones*. James Moriarty from *Sherlock*. A horrible Delores Umbridge of a person. It has to be someone whose opinion has no value to you whatsoever. Then the next time you have a negative thought, say it out loud but preface it with your character's name. For example, if you get stood up on a date, you might say, "Joffrey thinks I will die alone with fifty-seven cats." Then you'll think, *What does he know?* Joffrey doesn't operate on facts. Remember, you are not the problem. You were never the problem. The problem is the problem. So you might as well give it a name and a face, and keep on conquering.

But Am I Really Ready?

Making the journey from fangirl to fanwoman is no simple task. Throwing off addiction, fashioning new habits, and taming self-doubt are not things you can accomplish over a three-day weekend. Moving forward is about embracing both the Mulder and the Scully inside of you—you need the believer to reach for what seems impossible, but you also need the skeptic to be practical and help you move around roadblocks. Like any good ship, these two sides of you will conflict for a few seasons. But eventually they'll realize they can accomplish the most when they work together, and when they make out. Mmmm, make outs. Wait, what were we talking about? Oh yeah, life changes.

Even though I'm a therapist, I can't make you get up and start making changes any more than I can make NBC revive a decent Thursday night lineup. But I can teach you one of the most studied and practiced therapeutic techniques used today. It's called motivational interviewing (MI for short), and it's a simple but effective skill you can use on yourself and others to spark movement toward a significant goal. Developed by two clinical psychologists (thanks Miller and Rollnick!), MI helps people assess how ready they really are to change a habit, and it nudges them up the scale of self-improvement. It has helped those addicted to drugs or alcohol, people who want to lose weight, and folks struggling to get help for depression. It also works for your average fangirl who just wants to get her butt off the couch and finish her homework. Here's how.

Grab a piece of paper (get up, yo!) and fold it so you have four equal sections when you unfold it again. Label each section like this:

- Good Things about Not Changing

- Bad Things about Not Changing

- Good Things about Changing

- Bad Things about Changing

Now I want you to think of a behavior you'd like to change. It can be big or small, but it has to be something that won't come that easily to you. Maybe you want to check Tumblr less or read more books instead of fan fiction. Perhaps you're done spending your paycheck on merch or you'd like to rant less on the Internet. Or maybe you'd like to stop following an actress's every move as if she were a meteor hurtling toward Earth. Just pick one, and then fill out the categories. Experts advise that it's best to start with the good things about *not* changing the behavior (aka keeping the status quo) because in order to change we first have to acknowledge that we do what we do because we get something out of it. That twenty-eighth mini Snickers tastes good. That fifteenth rewatch of *Teen Wolf* is a wonderful escape. So let's pick a hypothetical behavior that needs to be cut out of day-to-day life. Let's say you want to stop checking the Idina Menzel hashtag on Instagram twenty-seven times a day. Here's what your chart might look like.

GOOD THINGS ABOUT NOT CHANGING	BAD THINGS ABOUT NOT CHANGING
• HER FACE THOUGH • Feeling up-to-date on news • Sharing photos with fangirl friends	• Feeling anxious when I can't check phone • Less time for work • Being rude when I'm socializing

GOOD THINGS ABOUT CHANGING	BAD THINGS ABOUT CHANGING
• Being a fan without feeling panicky • Enjoying my friends and family • Being a badass and getting stuff done	• Feeling like I'm missing fangirl news • Not being the 1st to share on social media • HER FACE THOUGH

Self-help guru Tony Robbins once said, "Change happens when the pain of staying the same is greater than the pain of change." If you'll look at the chart, you can see that if the bad things about not changing don't outweigh the bad things about changing, you're going to keep checking Instagram like a Broadway-lovin' maniac. So how do you tilt the balance?

The next step is a technique known as "scaling." And no, it does not involve mutating into a reptile to avoid all your problems. All you do is ask yourself, "On a scale of 1 to 10, how much do I want to change this behavior today?" And then you're honest with yourself. No lying! Here I'll start. On a scale of 1 to 10, when it comes to getting my booty off the couch today to do yoga, I'm like a solid 3. And 3 is not bad. It's better than 2, but I could be at 4. So rather than beating myself up for not being an Annie Edison energetic 10, I set my sights on the glamour of the 4.

How do I get from a 3 to a 4? That's up to me. Maybe I'll go change into workout clothes before I plop down in front of Netflix. Or I could fetch my mat while I start the next episode. Boom. I want it just a leetle bit more and am inching toward change. Knowing you're not ready is okay! Ask anyone how long it took them to lose weight, quit their horrible job, or change their spending habits, and the answer is usually years. Your job is to get yourself ready for change like your favorite celeb is going to show up at your house. Mop the floor one day. Blow up the air mattress the next. Pull out your finest *Star Trek* glassware. Much like winter, change is coming. And you want to be ready.

As you read through the book, you might want to refer back to the Good Things/Bad Things chart when you feel like I've highlighted a behavior you'd like to modify. Then scale your motivation and pay attention to the ones that rank higher than others. Then activate your powers like the BAMF that you are. Sally forth into the world, righting all wrong!

This concludes our fantastic journey through the fangirl brain! You've learned a few tricks, grown some mind grapes, and met our villain. Exit this way please, and mind the gap between this chapter and the next. Because next stop: Feels.

CHAPTER 2
ALL THE FEELS

I cannot handle a whole summer of the vaguest of *Downton Abbey* spoilers. Someone scale those privacy screens on the set and tell me what the hell is going on.

—RACHEL, THIRTY-ONE

I am not crazy. I am unique.

—SUZANNE WARREN, *ORANGE IS THE NEW BLACK*

So now you know a little bit about how the fangirl brain works. To quote legendary composer and lyricist Stephen Sondheim, "Isn't it nice to know a lot? And a little bit . . . not." Perhaps you're still wondering how on earth to tell if your fangirling is normal or unhealthy. Step one: throw the word *normal* out of your vocabulary. Because, lady, I wouldn't be writing this if I were normal, and you would not be reading it. I hope this book can help you celebrate your passionate personality, but learning to grow as a fangirl also requires you to slap a name and a face on some of the troublesome quirks you develop. So that's what we're going to do, as we explore the farthest reaches of feels.

I want to help you learn to deal with feels because I too have been past the point of extreme crey. I have felt that unspeakable anxiety when I wasn't the first person to post news on the Internet. I know the stomach-churning despair when you convince yourself that you will never write characters as well as a screenwriter. The disappointment when you look in the mirror and see a face that doesn't seem to look quite right for the bright lights. And I've known the quiet loneliness when you remember again and again that an actor who has impacted your life will never know you. I've shared the highs of fangirling with you, but I wouldn't have felt called to write this book if I had never sunk into the depths. And they go very, very deep, do they not?

This chapter is a guide to dealing with the feeliest of feels. I want to help you distinguish whether the fangirl symptoms you are experiencing are ones that require a little extra support and effort to address. To use fancy therapist language, we'll examine whether behaviors are syntonic or dystonic to the experience of being a fan. *Syntonic* means "having symptoms or emotions that are consistent with their environment," whereas *dystonic* describes uncommon behaviors. For example, if you sprint back and forth down the hallway of your house when you've bought plane tickets to Comic Con, this is a syntonic response. If you proceed to run out the door naked, up and down the hallway of your neighbor's house, while screaming in High Valyrian, this would probably be a dystonic response.

Being the unicorns that we are, each fangirl has different limits for what behaviors and emotions impair her day-to-day life. Some of you can laugh about your intense Sterek feelings and still show up to work and socialize with friends, while others are stuck spinning their wheels for a long time. To help you do a thorough feels assessment, I have created descriptions of a few of the conditions that are dystonic to the fangirl experience. It's likely that you may have found yourself in these situations or know friends who've exhibited these behaviors. In no way are they meant to be a clinical diagnosis. These descriptions are meant to make you laugh, but they might sober you up at bit as well and help you determine whether your behaviors need a little extra support to become less extreme and not take a toll on your health or personal life.

So browse through my Diagnostic Creys Manual (DCM)

and see if any of these apply to you. Note that the key criterion for each "diagnosis" is evidence that the behavior has interfered with your daily personal routine—work, school, relationships, family, etc. After you've read through the diagnoses, it's your turn to be the expert! I've provided you with a few fictional case studies about fangirl problem behaviors. See if you can diagnose these case studies based on the manual, and consider how you might recommend they improve their lives. In other words, be their fangirl mentor. Finally, I'll provide some info about the best ways to get started curing that intensity from the inside out. Because once you start erasing these dysfunctional behaviors from the map, you'll find greater joy in the fangirl life.

The Diagnostic Creys Manual, Version 1.0

BLINKING CURSOR SYNDROME. When a fangirl becomes so subsumed with writing fan fiction that she is unable or unwilling to produce any other work on her own. School papers, original fiction, and other forms of creative writing remain stalled or quickly transform into fic in midsentence (that is, You think you're comparing Hamilton and Jefferson's disparate views of government in that essay, but suddenly they start angsty yelling at each other).

BMW SYNDROME. When a fangirl becomes disoriented regarding a female celebrity and/or fictional character, not certain whether she wants the female to be her best friend, mother, or wife (hence BMW). To quote YouTuber Jenna Marbles, "I can't tell if I want to be you, or be on you." Ability to complete daily activities at work or school is impaired with this syndrome. Milder version is the **BMW Crush.**

CANON CONDUCT DISORDER TYPE 1. When a canonshipper frequently becomes visibly enraged at crackshippers within the same fandom. Symptoms include Tumblr tag bashing, leaving inappropriate and aggressive fan fiction reviews, and frequent whiny tweets. **Canon Conduct Disorder Type 2** is when a crackshipper frequently becomes visibly enraged at canonshippers within the same fandom. Symptoms same as Type 1. (Exceptions include *Rizzoli & Isles* shippers, who have an unalienable right to be furious.)

DEATH STAN DISORDER When a fangirl's favorite character dies on her favorite TV show, and she continues to watch only to make angry comments on social media about how the show was so much better with her favorite character. She is unable to ship any remaining characters and/or participate in other squee-related behavior. Behavior is diagnosable and dystonic only if it lasts for more than one season after the character dies. Similar to the diagnosis is **Departure Stan Disorder**, when a fangirl reacts with the same symptoms in response to a character's departure from a TV show. (Exceptions include any *Walking Dead* character for purposes of the author's own disillusionment and denial—Andreaaaaa!)

FILMOGRAPHY SYNDROME (FS) When a fangirl develops a celebrity crush and proceeds to marathon their entire filmography. Behavior is dystonic when daily activities and responsibilities are inhibited because the fangirl has devoted herself to watching every horrible Lifetime movie her fave has appeared in instead. FS can also grow out of other disorders (for example, **Death Stan Disorder with FS features**).

GIRL CRUSH PROJECTION DISORDER When a real life BAMF reminds a fangirl of a fictional character, the fangirl proceeds to obsess over the woman, imitating her appearance and actions, rather than seeking to build a healthy friendship or mentorship. Lines between fiction and reality blur more significantly than normal.

OBSESSIVE IMAGINATION DISORDER (OID) When a fangirl is constantly imagining scenarios regarding her OTP throughout the day, so that it inhibits the accomplishment of life responsibilities, including hygiene and basic social functioning. Variations include **OID with Domestic Scenario, OID with Smut Scenario, OID with Musical Accompaniment**, and **OID with Mixed Features**.

PASSIVE AGGRESSIVE POSSESSION SYNDROME (PAPS) When a fangirl's behavior indicates that she "owns" a character or TV show. She belittles others who make interpretations of character development that contradict

her own. She engages in frequent, nondirective ambiguous complaints on various social media outlets. Sometimes her aggression is more direct and is known as **PAPS with Aggressive Features**, which is called the **Gatekeeper Complex**.

POST SERIES FINALE DEPRESSION (PFSD)

Treat if four or more of the following symptoms persist for longer than two weeks: persistent incoherent mumbling of TV show's dialogue, frequent visible distress in public places, persistent Tumblr reblogging of painful gifs, dedication of significant amounts of time to writing AU fics of the show, frequent initiation of discussion involving character analysis with strangers, inability to initiate Netflix marathons of new TV shows, and/or aggressive outbursts at other fangirls who disagree with personal opinions.

PRESEASON ANXIETY DISORDER (PSAD)

Treat if three or more symptoms persist within three months of a season's beginning: persistent verbal and online speculation about upcoming plot, continual watching of trailers and reading of spoilers, marathoning previous episodes more than once within a hiatus, writing fic addressing speculation of upcoming plot, difficulty concentrating on other television shows and/or fangirl interests, engaging in ship wars.

SPONTANEOUS MISSIONARY SYNDROME

(SMS) When a fangirl responds so strongly to a new TV show, movie, book, etc. that she has an immediate, uncontrollable urge to convert other people to the interest. She argues more frequently, directing all conversation to the positives of the interests. If the interest is a TV show, she will often resort to holding friends and family members hostage until they have marathoned an inordinate number of episodes with her. Friends who are converted under this coercion may be diagnosed with **Spontaneous Missionary Stockholm Syndrome (SMSS)**.

So what do you think? Do any of these cases sound like you or a fangirl acquaintance? We've all had our filmography bouts or the postseason blues, but the difference between healthy fangirling and a feels attack is when you let your emotional re-activity deter you from living your daily life. While it might be easy to point at an Internet acquaintance and see the obvious

dysfunction, it can be a little more difficult to turn the focus on yourself and see what you'd like to change and what crusades you'd like to avoid in the future. To help you practice your diagnostic skills, I've included three fictional case studies for you. Read through them, and see if you can give a proper diagnosis from the DCM or come up with one on your own. Think about what you might say to these fangirls if they were your friends and how you might help them become conquering fanwomen.

CASE STUDY 1:
Beatrice and Benedict

Beatrice is a seventeen-year-old high school senior, and she lives a Benedict Cumberbatch appreciation life. She has watched *Sherlock* approximately twenty-five times and can quote every single line. She recently got into a fight with her best friend, Christina, who told her that she enjoys the 2009 *Star Trek* more than *Star Trek Into Darkness*. Beatrice has not replied to a single one of Christina's snapchats in a week, and she refuses to do so until Christina apologizes for her blatant ignorance. Things are also tense with Beatrice's parents, because like Benedict, she wants to take a gap year in between college to teach English in a Tibetan monastery and applies only to schools in the UK. Her parents think this is pretty freaking ridiculous, when her grades are good enough to get a merit scholarship to most U.S. universities.

All the Feels

Beatrice keeps a giant countdown calendar for the new *Sherlock* season in her bedroom. Every day she changes the number of days and hops up and down a little in excitement. She spends all of her evenings online, writing Johnlock drabbles and speculating about what will happen based on the most recent spoiler. She's also noticed recently that she has stopped watching her other favorite TV shows and struggles to be interested in the novels she has to read for her AP English class.

Beatrice finds herself writing nasty replies to Sherlock metas on Tumblr when she disagrees with them, and her follower count has been dropping every day. She's hoping that things will calm down once the new episodes start, but college applications are due between now and then. She's tried writing her essays, but she always ends up writing fic instead. How can she be expected to think about anything else when a new season is so close? And why can't the people in her life understand what it's like to be a fangirl?

1. Using the DCM, how would you describe Beatrice's feels?

2. How do you think she should handle the college application process?

3. How could Beatrice use her fangirl interests to help her meet her own goals?

4. If you were Beatrice's fangirl mentor, what other advice might you give her?

CASE STUDY 2:
Oh My Gillian

Sarah is a thirty-one-year-old high school chemistry teacher who loves her job almost as much as she loves *The X-Files*. She likes to brag that she was a Mulder and Scully shipper before fans had even invented the term *ship*. Sarah's husband had a job transfer last year, so she started teaching at a new school in a new city. Much to her surprise and joy, the chair of the science department looks and sounds exactly like Gillian Anderson, and Sarah CAN'T EVEN. Her husband found this very amusing the first time Sarah mentioned it to him, but now he is starting to worry. Sarah will snap pictures of the woman when she's not looking to show her online friends, and she talks about the other teacher endlessly.

Sarah, on the other hand, is thrilled by her mega girl crush on the older teacher. She has started buying clothes that are similar to hers and has even considered dyeing her hair a similar color. She has asked to sit in on the teacher's class several times during her free period, and she has started implementing many of the same techniques and reward strategies from the Gillian lookalike. She doesn't like that she's been arguing more with her husband when she doesn't want to go out on the weekends. She'd rather stay at home and marathon *The Fall* or go through her *X-Files* DVDs.

"If you admire her so much," Sarah's husband asks, "then why don't you try to be her friend? You're just as amazing a teacher as she is."

Sarah's eyes don't leave the TV screen as she replies, "Don't be ridiculous. She would never want to be my friend."

1. Using the DCM, how would you describe Sarah's feels?

2. How do you think Sarah could better handle her girl crush?

3. How could Sarah use her fangirl interests to help her meet her own goals?

4. If you were Sarah's fangirl mentor, what advice might you give her?

CASE STUDY 3:
Annoying Is the New Black

In a million years, Hannah would never have thought she'd get so excited about prison. A twenty-two-year-old college senior and sociology major, she recently became obsessed with the show *Orange Is the New Black*. For the past year, Hannah has been volunteering at a local halfway house for women exiting prison, and many of the stories on the show resonated with her. She also quickly realized that none of her friends outside of the Internet watched the show, and she instantly made it her duty to get everyone she knew to watch all the episodes.

For a few hours one day, Hannah camps herself on the futon with her roommate to watch some of the show. "Do you want to watch another episode?" she asks her eagerly. "Who's your favorite character? Is it Taystee? What about Maritza? Isn't Piper the wooooorst? I'm so glad they got rid of Larry. I can't decide whether I really ship Morello and Nichols or not." She frowns in disappointment as her roommate yawns and says she needs to finish a math problem set. "But I threw my pie for you!" she shouts after her.

At the end of her sociology class the next week, Hannah makes an announcement to everyone that they need to watch the show. "It will change your life," she explains to her very confused professor. That night Hannah gets into a huge argument with her long-distance girlfriend when she refuses to Skype-watch the show with her. "You don't care about me if you won't watch this show!" Hannah shouts before hanging up on her.

Staring at her cell phone, Hannah gets the urge to call her mom. "I'm coming home this weekend and you're going to watch something with me," she explains to her mother. "Pick me up at four tomorrow."

1. Using the DCM, how would you describe Hannah's feels?

2. How do you think she could address her frustrations with her girlfriend?

3. How could Hannah use her fangirl interests to help meet her own goals?

4. If you were Hannah's fangirl mentor, what advice might you give her?

The Cure for Your Creys?

So now it's time to roll out the confetti cannons as I reveal the super, secret, magic fix for all your fangirling dysfunction. Right? So you can plow your way into your next binge-watch without any harm to your personal life. Right, right? Sadly I am a muggle therapist, and there is no magic here. Only truths. And the truth is that if you want to fangirl your way to success, you have to fundamentally change the way you treat other people and the way you treat yourself. No short cuts, no Five Easy Steps! Just living.

As we learned in the last chapter, the fangirl operates as she does largely because of anxiety. Your life is full of anxiety whether you are a *Once Upon a Time* fan or not. A final exam, rush hour traffic, and having to call someone on the phone like an adult are all culprits. So are second movies in trilogies and waiting for fanfic reviews. We are destined for a life of stressors because we are humans, and part of being human is feeling broken, getting scared, and craving love and attention. The good news is that being human is also about healing, comforting, and loving ourselves and others. So our task on this planet is to figure out how we can balance out the scary parts of this story with the wonderful ones. To add comedy to the tragedy.

When we commit ourselves to this task, by helping ourselves and accepting help from others, our anxiety can become manageable. We can finally poke our heads above the water and say, "This isn't so bad."

Real change is an inside and outside process. We have to address how we treat both others and ourselves both on and offline, and that means being kind to our tiny unicorn selves and to others. Kindness isn't a prescription your doctor can write. It's only something you can consciously wake up each day and decide to live. If you're operating defensively, rejecting others' opinions, and stirring up conflict, then you should expect to be anxious. I'm a culprit of this myself sometimes. Maybe I find myself getting all ragey at immature Internet folks, wondering, "Why is everyone acting like a teenager?" Only to realize that the person pissing me off *is* a teenager. In a fandom, you are responsible for only your own actions and reactions. You are not responsible for policing a fifteen-year-old boy's opinions about Skyler White. As long as the Internet reigns supreme, it will always be easier to get upset with someone than to step back a second and consider what kindness can accomplish. When we're not concerned with being right or serving a smackdown, amazing things can happen.

When it comes to our internal evolution, *Treat yo self* is a phrase we all know whether we are *Parks and Recreation* fans or not. But I find myself shaking my head sometimes when I see fangirls talk about coping with anxiety. Because all too often, we conflate coping methods with the practices that actually get us all riled up. If you're only distracting yourself from the stresses of life, then sooner or later it's going to find you like an angry Internet troll. When you watch ten Channing Tatum movies in a row, you are not being kind to yourself. When you are refreshing your email every ten seconds for fic reviews, you are not being kind to yourself. These behaviors might feel rewarding in the moment, but they are not the self-care that you need. Taking a step back to breathe is essential. Call a friend you haven't spoken to in a while. Put a block on a website you obsess over. Read a book. It wouldn't be completely ridiculous to have a self-care plan in place for when you decide to marathon a show or you have a potentially painful TV season on the horizon. Steven Moffat sure as hell isn't going to take care of you. So you better step up and do it yourself.

When you jerk the rug of distraction out from under yourself, you have to replace it with a better way of dealing. You begin to use all your senses to practice living in the moment. You're shutting screens off before bed. You're willing to engage your own scary brain instead of checking your phone at a red light, and you're ready to start communicating with people who epitomize your rage triggers. You are even willing to talk it out with a professional when you need it.

I want to give you permission to treat yourself. To binge-watch a great TV show (*Catastrophe*, anyone?) when you need to de-stress. The goal isn't to stop distracting yourself—this is an evolutionary mechanism that helps us survive the plot twists of life. The goal is to start engaging your anxiety in addition to distracting. It might feel like you will die if you miss an episode or a cast interview, but you'll feel freer without that sense of urgency. You'll find that when you do dive into fictional worlds, it's more about taking a vacation than it is about escaping your mind like a refugee rushing for the border. But how do you do this? You do a little brain sculpting.

The Mindful Fangirl

When you start learning to pay attention to your feels as a fangirl, you develop a sort of extra superhero sense. Though Agent Phil Coulson might not be calling you up, this remarkable ability allows you to change the physical structure of the brain itself, long after you leave childhood. Often called mindfulness, this ability allows the fangirl to slowly gain control over her reactions rather than instantaneously smashing the keyboard or diving under a blanket. Here are a few ways you can develop mindfulness.

SEE YOUR FEELS AT WORK. When you see intense fangirl emotions as wires in your brain instead of a character flaw, you lower anxiety. So when someone dies on *American Horror Story,* instead of thinking, "I am Ryan Murphy trash," you might observe, "Hey, that really lit up my anxiety response!" Seeing your anxiety as a process rather than a negative label you slap on yourself tunes you in to what's happening when you're stuck in traffic or avoiding an email from your professor. It also makes you a less reactive person over time. If you don't want to think of your worries or panic as wires, you can use other metaphors. I like to think of them as boats flopping up and down as they cruise the harbor of my mind. There goes the S. S. *Catastrophizing!*

DON'T "SHOULD" YOURSELF. *Should* isn't usually a motivating word, and we get mentally stuck when we start bossing ourselves to shape up, do better, and calm the hell down. Practicing awareness means observing emotions and reactions like a naturalist, with respect and curiosity. When we try to cage them and tame them without seeking to understand them, we forget that they can lead us toward real change. Maybe you'd rather not be so anxious waiting for someone to like your post on Tumblr, but here you are, so you might as well examine your emotion rather than beating yourself up about it. "If you have a fight with yourself," asks psychiatrist and mindfulness expert Dan Siegel, "Who can win?" The simple act of being curious about your brain makes your response to stress more flexible. Yes, the stress response is annoying when triggered by the slightest thing, but it's helped us survive as a species and get through Nina Dobrev's departure from *Vampire Diaries.* So show a little respect!

THINK BEFORE YOU TWEET. Social media culture does not lend itself to real reflection. The itch of the fingers to tweet a complaint or text your fury can switch off the ability to be thoughtful. And when we reach out only to Internet folks we know who will agree with us, we become less empathetic. Emotionally intelligent humans hit the pause button to gauge a situation with their prefrontal cortex. But if you're always racing to be the first one to have a hilariously ragey comment on the Internet, then you'll just get wound up tighter and tighter. And before you know it, you've exploded vicious rhetoric on some poor Bethyl shipper on Tumblr who never saw it coming.

LEAN IN, BABY! Many fangirls spend a significant amount of energy trying to avoid negative emotions. But you should be the Sheryl Sandberg of your own anxiety and lean into it. In his book *Mindsight*, Siegel uses the metaphor of a river to describe how your brain moves along with the flow of life. One side of the riverbank represents the dangers of "rigidity," where you feel stuck or unable to escape a depressed mood. On the other side is "chaos," where you sometimes feel agitated or ragey because events are outside of your control. If you are willing to be more observant about how your fangirl brain and body react, then the banks of the river grow wider apart and the less likely you are to career headlong into the shore like the final level of *Oregon Trail*. In short, you'll lean forward, enjoy the journey, and be less pissed about someone's comment that season 8 of *Supernatural* was brilliant.

These practices will not be easy at first. Slowly but surely, you can fashion a fangirl brain that is aware of itself and amazed by its complexity and powers of compassion. You'll enjoy the feels, but you won't be controlled by them.

Destination Fanwoman

None of these suggestions imply that you need to stop fangirling. If you're thinking that right about now, then go back to page 1 and start over. Don't stop believing and don't stop feeling passionate about fiction. Instead, start *using* it to engage. You may be wondering, "How do I give my girl crush or my favorite show attention without being anxious? Isn't that the very definition of being a fangirl?" It depends on which side of yourself is taking the wheel. (Jesus can't do this part; this is on you, bae.) Is it the immature part of you that wants approval desperately? The piece of you that wants to forget about those deadlines or that important email? Or is it the part of you that is passionate about the kind of role you want to play in your own life?

When I watch TV with a strong sense of what I value and who I want to be, I am less likely to make the compromises and crave the distractions that generate anxiety. Strong fictional characters and inspiring stories aren't smushed into a blob of feelings I stuff inside myself to fill in the gaps created by all the should be's and could be's that are just too scary to contemplate. Instead, they are the colors I use to paint a picture of what my life could be. What a life *better* than fiction could entail. So that is a question you must ask yourself: Am I crazy about a character because he or she is a convenient distraction from what is missing in my own life? Or am I crazy about a character because there is a giant blinking sign over her head that says THIS WAY. Because when you follow in that direction, you're headed toward something quite different from and quite better than being a fangirl. Something I call fanwoman.

Now that we've descended into the depths, it's time to rise up and move forward. For the rest of the book, we'll explore how to use your fangirl loves to conquer like a true heroine. I can't think of a better way to start that journey than some hardcore lady crushing.

CHAPTER 3
THE GIRL CRUSH

I just want to watch a TV show with badass and inspirational middle-aged women. Is that too much to ask?

—**LAUREN, TWENTY-FOUR**

It's a new pop culture trend where young women desperately in need of female role models call other girls they look up to "Mom."

—**CHANEL #3, *SCREAM QUEENS***

Take a woman. Dress her in impossibly fabulous clothes, prep her hair and makeup for three hours, and gift her with a brilliant script, and a not so surprising thing occurs: other women begin to worship her. When we admire another female in fiction, we find ourselves so deep in emotions that we tend to forget the entire army of experts hiding behind her perfection. Or the reality that she sprang from the head of a writer, like Athena born from Zeus.

The fangirl may not live on a compound in southern Utah, but she usually has at least a dozen wives at her disposal. We contract lady crushes faster than we can immunize ourselves because who doesn't need another fictional heroine who kicks ass with perfect hair? If you unraveled my heart and slapped it on a coffee table, it would read like a geological strata map of lady loves. Three decades of layers where each girl crush shaped a significant part of my identity construction. Only to suddenly be dethroned by a new love who blasts from out of nowhere like a fiery tornado of sass and hairporn.

To my young brain, any confident and accomplished woman, real or fictional, was a goddess walking on Earth. If Murphy Brown could get away with firing a thousand secretaries and popping out a baby without a man or Dan Quayle's permission, then I sure as hell could beat my male competitors in the county spelling bee. My mother died when I was nineteen, so as a young woman, I continued to take my cues from the powerhouses on my television screen. For better or worse, they each influenced the parade of quirks that constructed my adult personality.

The reality is that there is a whole catalog of lady loves. Some are superficial, and others are lifeboats. They seem to arrive always when we need them, at the turning points of our own life stories or when deficits exist. So when a new girl crush looms, stop to gather some information before you dismiss it. There are many kinds, but here's a small sampler from the buffet of girl crushes a fangirl may develop.

THE HAIRPORN CRUSH.

Don't be fooled by the initial innocence of mooning over a female's hair, clothing, face, or general appearance. A good plot is appreciated on a show, but if there's amazing hair and fashion, we're likely to keep showing up week after week no matter what. Perhaps the most common type of crush, in many ways it can also be the most devastating. In extreme cases, the fangirl may seek to completely replicate the person's hairstyle or fashion sense. Or she simply might be debilitated with tears. This crush is most enjoy-

HAIRNADO WARNING!

9 PM EST
on a screen
near you

able when you have a buddy who can text you pictures of Kate Walsh during boring work meetings. But she can also tell you to snap out of it when you're being too cray cray, or remind you that your bank account is not Blair Waldorf's.

THE MOM CRUSH. A rarer breed of crushing, this one occurs when the fangirl projects some of her family feels onto a celebrity or fictional character. While it can be healthy and even productive to admire the qualities of an older female, calling your fave "Mom" can be problematic. For example, maybe Lorelai Gilmore is the mom you always wanted, but dwelling on a fantasy won't get you very far. The best solution is to dedicate some time to working on your own family relationships and to develop mutually beneficial female friendships with older women.

THE FRIEND CRUSH. Fictional characters are often adorable dorks, so it's no wonder that we wouldn't mind adding them to our list of friends. A fangirl might even have imaginary conversations with them in her head (or out loud, because yes, we all have conversations with ourselves out loud sometimes). If you're a sucker for the friend crush, I'd encourage you to find a fangirl friend who admires the same qualities in a character and create your own antics. In other words, turn off the TV and go find the Cristina Yang to your Meredith Grey. The beautiful tropical fish Ann Perkins to your Leslie Knope. The Taystee to your Poussey. Okay, that sounded weird.

THE ACTUAL CRUSH. Many fangirls will share how fandom was a much needed introduction for them to begin or continue to explore their own sexuality. Perhaps physical attraction to a female (real life or fictional) was another piece of the puzzle to help define themselves to the world and to feel comfortable with their sexuality. It's important, however, to never make assumptions about a person's sexual orientation based on a fictional crush. So if you're wondering why your lesbian friend is crying about Tom Hiddleston or why your straight friend refers to Jennifer Lawrence as her wife, just let her be.

THE NINJA CRUSH. Sometimes we see fictional ladies performing the most badass moves imaginable, like blowing stuff up, or doing magic like WHOA. That doesn't make us necessarily want to enlist in the military, join the CIA, or buy a samurai sword, but we can channel that energy to do our homework or stand up to our boss by watching and admiring these insane ladies. A ninja crush can be a great tool to rev you up in the morning, so if you need to watch Bellatrix Lestrange smoke people, Beatrix Kiddo bust her way out of a grave, or Michonne from *The Walking Dead* decapitate thirty-one zombies, then by all means go for it.

THE MENTOR CRUSH. Some of us huddle around female characters who are career conquerors and don't apologize for it. Perhaps it's the way Annalise Keating commands a classroom, how Dana Scully masters a male-dominated workplace, or how lady detective Phryne Fisher catches criminals without besmirching her whites. Mentors are notorious for what my friend Lauren coined OFB, outrageously fancy behavior. Personally I'm entranced when an older lady glares over her reading glasses or leans on a conference room chair like a lioness. We're also captivated by the wisdom that floats out of a woman's mouth and makes us stop and take notes. Mentor crushes are perhaps the most useful, but that doesn't mean they can't be the most feels inducing as well.

THE SITUATION ROOM CRUSH. Sometimes two or more of these types of crushes can combine, morphing into an insatiable feelings monster. No amount of screencaps, fan fiction, headcanon, filmography, and YouTube interviews is enough. I call this state of feels "the Situation Room." Used in a sentence: "Kathleen can't hang out with you this week, because she's in the Situation Room." I've had three of these crushes in my life. Emma Pillsbury (Jayma Mays) from *Glee*, Laura Roslin (Mary McDonnell) from *Battlestar Galactica*, and Diane "Queen of Everything" Lockhart (Christine Baranski) from *The Good Wife*.

The Situation Room is both a blessing and a curse. On a scale of 1 to 10, 1 being passing a kidney stone and 10 being winning the lottery, it feels like a 73 and a -37 at the same time. It's like being in love, only you don't have to shave your legs or form coherent sentences because the object of your affection doesn't know you exist. Being from the Internet myself, I have seen the very worst of the worst that can happen when a fangirl gets emotionally locked in the Situation Room. Admiration is nice, but when you compete with nemeses for best fan website, or when you actively stalk a celebrity, you may find yourself a few miles past the last rest stop for sanity.

The Psychology of the BAMF

Maybe you're thinking about your own girl crushes or a friend's, and wondering, "Is Hayley Atwell really worth the emotional energy?" This is a relevant question when you consider all the things you could be doing with your life. The major dilemma with the girl crush is that it functions as a gateway drug to more lovely ladies. When we admire a character, this creates a temporary high. Like any addiction, it's a glorious, fleeting rush of feelings that must be replicated as often as possible to reap the benefits. Just like a drug addict develops a tolerance to a substance, it takes more and more stimulus to achieve the initial level of girl crush high. Thus to satisfy our cravings, we get too busy trying to replicate those intense feelings to take the girl crush any further than our initial, automatic response. We get caught, and we never think about what a girl crush represents or the potential it holds for changing our behaviors on a deep, person-centered level. In other words, you're too busy defending Nicki Minaj to Internet haters to stop and use some of that gumption you're admiring and expending to follow your own dreams.

But if you're patient or lucky enough, sometimes a brilliant Halley's Comet of a thing will happen. You start to absorb some of the characteristics you admire in the crush. Perhaps you catch yourself before you unnecessarily apologize to a co-worker, or you begin to stand up for yourself in a romantic relationship. When I think about all the bold leaps I've taken in my life with the help of my girl crushes, the is-it-worth-it scale begins to tip even. I call this phenomenon the power of the BAMF.

In the past few years, fangirls requisitioned the term BAMF to describe badass women who dominate our televisions, movie screens, books, and stages. It's kind of a feminist appropriation of the sexist acronym for badass mother effer. She comprises both feminine qualities and the stuff of the gods. She's never interested in people pleasing or sitting around blaming others for the problems in her life, and the sassiest retort is always on standby, in case her martial arts or her intelligence aren't deadly enough for the given occasion. Or to say it in fangirl, YAS QUEEN YAS.

BAMFy women also exhibit a clear sense of identity. They don't give a frak what other people think, and they will stop at nothing to accomplish their goals. They have zero time for gossiping or feeling jealous. You see them smackdown trolls in true Amy Schumer fashion, and fangirls ride the high of their triumph. But the next day maybe you show up at school or work drowning in anxiety and worrying about what other people think. You whine and get downright spiteful when you interact with other fangirls. Essentially, sometimes you do exactly the opposite of what you elevate. Perhaps you experience extreme stress over the smallest of things, like not getting enough reviews on a fanfic or missing a midnight release of a movie. So what hope is there to lift your focus above your worries and fears when you face the big decisions in life, like your job, school, and relationship choices?

You'd think that as much time as the average fangirl spends studying and giffing the subject of her affection, that she would be a veritable expert at being an A+ BAMF. But if you spend three seconds engaged in a fandom, you'll find preschool-level maturity rearing its ugly head. Why don't we gradually become more like the women we admire? Are we to be stuck eternally in the classroom of badassery, never graduating? We're too timid to apply for our dream job, much less rule the entire universe or slice open a herd of zombies.

There's a one-word explanation: anxiety. The scarlet A of the fangirl, anxiety is the driving force behind the intensity of our addiction. We might worship *Firefly's* Zoë Washburne because we love a good story and appreciate a real heroine, but all the motivation and energy gets wasted because we're stuck in the mud of anxiety, spinning our wheels. This anxiousness can look different depending on the fangirl. Some of us are rapid cyclers who go through new, intense crushes faster than Shonda Rhimes can create a television show. Others get stuck on one woman for years, getting so entrenched with running a fandom and "owning" a character that they forget what even drew them to the person in the first place. Regardless, in the haze of hair-porn and headcanon, we can lose sight of what can be motivating as we flail about in the anxiety of it all.

It's "canon" with one "N"

Some people are just more anxious creatures than others. A lot of factors outside our control influence our ability to be a calm force in the midst of chaos. Our genetics, families, and environment are random cards that are dealt to us. But like our favorite characters, we must decide how we play them. We are all capable of building a clearer sense of who we are. We can make decisions that reflect our real passions and beliefs and are not about pleasing other people, but it requires a bit of strategizing. So let's look at some advanced bold moves.

Strategies for Becoming a Strong Female Character

Learning to be a strong female character means developing a strategy for dealing with all kinds of people and crises. In our quest to journey through life, midseason hiatuses, and the Internet, fangirls are known to react in a number of ways to stress. Some of these strategies are mature, and some of them, eh . . . not so much. If you start paying attention to how you interact with other people, you'll see that there are clear signposts you can look for on the path from fangirl to fanwoman, from harumph to BAMF. This transformation starts when you ask yourself three questions.

1. How do I handle conflict?

2. How do I not get caught in the middle?

3. How do I not run away?

Remember that *Sesame Street* bit when a huffing and puffing Grover ran back and forth, teaching you the difference between neeeeear and faaaaaar? Being a BAMF requires knowing which direction to move when you run into anxiety. You have to know when to be near, when to be far, and when to not get caught in the middle. In fact, I'd argue that most character development in fiction happens when a person figures out these strategies. So let's learn them, shall we?

HOW DO I HANDLE CONFLICT? A fangirl is usually an anxious creature, and she has numerous stressors in her life. One way we react to this anxiety is to engage in conflict with others. In fact, if you're in a fandom, you may find that you thrive on conflict as much as you complain about it to others. In other words, you love to stir up crap. Saying "I'm right and let me explain to you how you're always wrong in your wrongness," feels good in the moment, especially when other people rally around you, but it's a temporary solution. The power is fleeting, and you have to replicate the drama over and over again. Extreme shippers tend to be the worst at this, and they usually don't realize all of their righteous anger is more about them feeling less anxious than it is about winning the latest Destiel/Wincest skirmish.

Does a BAMF avoid all conflict? No. But when she engages in an argument or a disagreement, it's because she is standing up for her beliefs and representing her true self to the world. She can remain calm and objective when she talks to those who might disagree with her, and she doesn't give the trolls her time of day. She knows that the best revenge is living well, and that's exactly what she does.

HOW DO I NOT GET CAUGHT IN THE MIDDLE?

To become a strong female character, the fangirl must avoid threesomes with the same fervor she uses to complain about the most dreaded plot device since the dawn of time—the love triangle. When I use the word *triangle*, however, I'm not talking about your Katniss-Gale-Peeta angst. I'm using a therapy term that describes how two people ease the tension in their relationship by honing in on a third. For example, a friendship might form because two fangirls dislike the same person in their fandom. Women in particular are all too quick to entertain ourselves by complaining about other people, and that my friends, is a triangle. Alternatively, we might find ourselves pulled into drama to settle conflicts between friends or to take sides.

While it might feel good to whine about a person who annoys the hell out of us or to get sucked into squabbles, ultimately it distracts us from our goals in life. They are unnecessary side plots that have nothing to do with our character arc. Strong women are not about the triangle. If they have a problem with somebody, they confront the person head on. They're too busy running and saving the world to talk smack or complain about other people, and their relationships are built on positive commonalities rather than hater tactics.

HOW DO I NOT RUN AWAY? It's a true fangirl instinct to want to put an ocean-size distance between you and someone who bothers you. When we're uncomfortable or anxious, we cut people off. We block, mute, or unfollow, and sometimes we take that instinct and apply it to real life. Facing potential disagreement or disapproval is just too much, so we fall out of contact with people who are important to us or could teach us something.

If fictional ladies never confronted conflict, we'd all change the channel out of boredom. Dorothy Zbornak never would have had a witty reply. Leslie Knope never would have challenged her moron city council members. Look at any Emmy- or Oscar-winning scene, and I guarantee you that what you'll find is the exact opposite of bolting. BAMFs stand firm, even when it's difficult, because they're ready and able to show the world who they are and what they want. Does that mean you need to be pen pals with every asshole you come across on the Internet? No. What it does mean is that characters in your life don't get replaced as often as a DADA instructor. Your relationships will survive disagreements, your career will survive negative feedback, and your fandom life will survive the stray conflict.

I also want to be clear that being girl-crush worthy isn't like being a droid or a Vulcan. The bravest women let themselves be vulnerable in relationships. They admit when they are wrong, and they even sometimes cry in the bathroom at work. You can't turn off your emotions, but you can be calm and thoughtful before you respond to a situation. You can wait for the clarity that happens when you take steps to address your anxiety. And that clarity is about acting out your own story and pushing toward challenges, rather than being tossed about by the whims and demands of others.

So let's review:

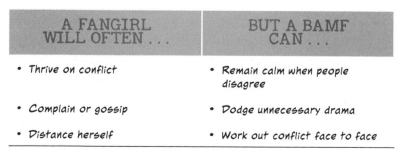

A FANGIRL WILL OFTEN . . .	BUT A BAMF CAN . . .
• Thrive on conflict	• Remain calm when people disagree
• Complain or gossip	• Dodge unnecessary drama
• Distance herself	• Work out conflict face to face

From Ingénue to Khaleesi

Learning to make bold moves is a life-long endeavor, and like the journey of a true Khaleesi, crises and setbacks are inevitable along the way. We'll hear all sorts of advice from all kinds of advisers, and we'll feel the pull to please them, lose direction, and forsake our true beliefs. Essentially, we forget that we have the power to walk through fire unscathed. We look to fiction, but then we remember that our lives and words aren't scripted. Real life is one giant improv show. You don't have an entire team mapping out possible one-liners on a whiteboard before you go on a first date. The problems in your life don't form a neat little arc that comes to a close every year. You don't have makeup and hair prep for a two-minute conversation with your best friend. We're just flailing about on our own, and we just really, really want people to like us. Even on the Internet. *Especially* on the Internet. So in our quest to be bold, we're bound to royally screw things up from time to time.

So knowing all of this, can we really glean anything constructive from people who don't even exist? Yes! A thousand times yes. As the great Margaret Atwood said, "You're never going to kill storytelling, because it's built into the human plan. We come with it." Humans and storytelling are a package deal because we carry with us whatever gets us through the day, girl crushes included. When I think of all the ladies who have stood out above the others, all the Tami Taylors and the Miranda Baileys and the Minerva McGonagalls, I see stories about women who do what is right whenever everyone else would advise them to take the easy road. I feel inspired in a way that has little to do with ninja moves or sass and everything to do with living a life of true character.

There is no secret formula for becoming a BAMF, but the truth of the transformation boils down to this: Courageous women make decisions that do not cave to what is convenient or petty. Similarly, when you model your life after the way of the BAMF, you'll know who you are and what you value, and you won't apologize for it. How do you begin? The process starts when you're ready to climb up out of the trenches, to give up putting down others or letting yourself feel less worthy. It is a process that requires showing up daily and making many mistakes. If it were super easy, then it wouldn't be a story worth sticking with for the long haul. Maybe you're not ready quite yet, and if you were scaling your commitment like we learned in an earlier chapter, you'd be a 2 or a 3. So let's take a look at some strategies you can use and people you can have in your camp to begin your long yet captivating journey toward the throne.

The Mentorship

Self-improvement never has to be a solo endeavor. You're going to have a hell of a lot more fun and encouragement if you're willing to let others share the road with you. Working on yourself requires a lot of private reflection and effort, but it can also be about casting women (or men) in your life who are examples of maturity, kindness, and yes, badassery. So if you're feeling a little sad that you'll never have Olivia Benson as a boss, I suggest you put out an open casting call for a real-life lady crush. Or what a regular person might call a mentor.

Asking someone to be your mentor can be pretty freaking terrifying when you don't even like to order a pizza without using an app (why thank you Domino's, I *would* like to open the tracker now). But the reality is that most people love talking about their lives and careers, and most people older than you would love to impart some wisdom. What is more flattering than hearing someone say they'd like to model a part of their life after yours?

How do you ask someone to be your mentor? Take out a Craigslist ad? "Baby unicorn seeks flawless HBIC to cry about." Nah. You certainly can't slip them a paper that says, "Will UB my personal lady hero, check yes or no." Just present the facts: You have a passion in common with them, and you'd love to discuss it. I've emailed writers and said, "Hey, I want to talk to you about writing." I've emailed editors and said, "Hey, I want to write for you, so how do we make this happen?" With older acquaintances I've been more honest and admitted I was literally fangirling over them. It all depends on the relationship.

A real-life mentorship takes time and effort, and the human quality of the relationship might prove surprising to those of us who idealize people we don't know. Sometimes people will disappoint you, and you'll see that every lady has flaws. But having someone actively root for you, someone invested in your success, is such a priceless gift. As much as you might want her to, a fictional lady can never give you that. Fostering courage through fictional characters is great. In fact, it's my favorite thing about being a fangirl. But having a relationship that's a two-way street is even better, because the only thing tougher than being a fearless woman on paper or on screen is being one in real life. A true mentorship is likely to fill the little Mindy Kaling–shaped hole in your heart that just wants somebody who can high-five you and help you along the way. So go get ya one!

From Crey to Slay

You know how engineers can make a car run on French fry grease? Well a girl crush is like a feels-powered spaceship that can power your journey from a waifish fangirl to a full-on fanwoman. So you can drown in your tears or you can dump them in the gas tank to do some conquering. To gather some fuel, let's do another quick exercise. Grab a pen and some paper, and take a minute to list as many of your fictional girl crushes as you can. Then glance over the list, and circle the top four for whom you have the most feels. Don't worry, I won't tell the others. Now brainstorm some of the common characteristics that these four women have, and choose the ones that appeal to you the most. Think about what would happen if you shoved some of these personality traits into a cooler and transplanted them into your own life. What would you be doing differently? How would your work be different and how would your relationships change?

If you'd like more practice, here are a few other girl crush techniques I've used over the years and a few recommended by friends to get you started.

BAMF TALISMAN. A talisman is an object thought to have magical properties that would provide luck or ward off evil. While there's no magic to the BAMF talisman, it does induce a sort of placebo effect where you draw out power you already have. It can be as simple as a piece of jewelry representing a girl crush or a mug with your favorite one-liner from your favorite lady. My talisman is a tiny katana necklace like the sword Michonne carries on *The Walking Dead*. I don't wear it for fear that I might actually puncture a lung in a staff meeting, but I clutch it before a job interview or an important presentation and tell myself, as Michonne once said, "My s— never stopped being together."

GOLD STAR CHART. Remember in elementary school when your mom or teacher gave you a gold star sticker every time you tied your own shoes or kept your mouth shut? Well now you can bring that joy back. I used to make a weekly gold star sticker chart of all the mundane but necessary things I want to accomplish each day, like flossing, exercising, and making my bed.

The problem with daily habits though, is that they suck. So slap a photo of Retta on your weekly to-do list, and voilà. Your motivation isn't just to get stuff done anymore. You see the photo and think, "Oh my God. If I don't pack my lunch and save money, then I'll never be that fabulous." Forget whether this is actually true. The screencap makes it true.

HEALTHY GUILTING! As a therapist, I sometimes tell clients that guilt is not a helpful emotion. As a fangirl, I actively ask my friends to use my girl crushes to guilt me, and vice versa. After all, Laura Roslin found time to go to the gym when she was president of the universe and dying of cancer, so what excuse do I really have? If they can do it, so can you. So asking yourself, "What Would Melinda May Do?" might inspire you to muster the energy to chase after your goals. With a little bit of creativity, you can repurpose passion for a girl crush into something that gets your ass in gear, and then there's no telling what you can do.

THE BAMF CODE. In your quest toward awesomeness, I recommend creating some sort of mission statement or a code to live by. Values that guide you when anxiety takes the lead and tries to make you dance in a different direction. Your code should reflect your own goals, but I think that pulling from the lovely fictional ladies (and men) you admire is an excellent place to start. It would not be surprising if many of your girl crushes had similar traits. Here is my code.

1. I will take responsibility for my own feels and distress

2. I can be a resource to people without being responsible for them

3. I will not adjust my values and goals to seek approval from others

4. I will not apologize for taking care of myself

5. I will not run away screaming from situations that are an opportunity for growth as a BAMF

6. Slay, queen, slay

When you set aside the hairporn and the heels and tease out everything I love about my favorite female characters, these are really the traits that shine above all the others. They are women who are willing and ready to take responsibility for their lives, control their fates, and foster happy and healthy relationships. Maybe your code would look different from mine, so don't be afraid to sketch out a few quick ideas. Then start testing your code among friends, family, and complete strangers. For example, what would it look like for you to take responsibility for your own distress when someone disagrees with you about your Huddy feelings? When someone steals your gif set? Doesn't reply to your Tweet? Every day is an arena for defining yourself. To make choices based on principle rather than fear or anxiety. To BAMF it out.

Remember, becoming a woman worth girl crushing over is a multiseason plot. Often what appeals to us about fictional stories is the progression from timid creature to the conquering queen. When you begin to make decisions that reflect your true self, you are building your BAMF story. That story arc may crash and burn from time to time, but we dust the flaming debris off ourselves, we stand up, and we start acting from the inside out.

CHAPTER 4
THE HAIR AND THE GLARE

I don't like how tightly they are curling Mellie's hair on *Scandal* right now, and it's the worst thing that has ever happened to me.

—AMANDA, THIRTY-ONE

I am relieved since now I know exactly where I stand. Somewhere below your precious little label and your stupid, perfect hair.

—JULIETTE BARNES, *NASHVILLE*

Once upon a time, a very confusing time in my life, I was in the *Glee* fandom (cue flashback harps). A naive ingénue in the world of Internet fandom, I thought that I was just enjoying a television show. Little did I know that I would soon embark on the greatest human experiment since *The Real World*: THE NO PANTS CHALLENGE.

When I first started watching *Glee*, I become enamored with costume designer Lou Eyrich's wardrobe selections for the female characters. In particular, Emma Pillsbury's colorful cardigans, vintage sweater clips, and Mary Jane heels completely captured my heart and my bank account. A little bit of Internet searching connected me with Danielle, a fabulous lady who had created a website cataloging everything that Emma wore on the show, even vintage pieces for sale on eBay. I was hooked. For the next year of my life, I taught myself how to ID clothing on TV shows and became the Boba Fett of enamel flower brooches. I learned that discontinued Anthropologie cardigans are the most coveted treasures, and the great hunt connected me with a group of amazing women with similar passions.

In this fashion community, we started to joke about how Emma Pillsbury never wore pants on the show. Looking in my closet one morning, surveying my eBay prey, I realized that I had so many beautiful clothes that I overlooked at home for the comfort of jeans and T-shirts. I often wore the same pair of dress pants with holes in the pockets to work every day and rarely stepped into the heels I was so fond of buying. *Why am I so afraid of standing out?* I asked myself. Could I go a week without wearing pants or jeans, sticking just to dresses and skirts? A month? A whole year?

It turned out that I could. I blogged about the experience and made many more friends. The No Pants Challenge was an opportunity for me to come out of the fangirl closet for a while, and lo and behold, nobody made fun of me. People were genuinely interested in my progress and cheered me on my pantless journey. Fast-forward six years. Now I wear pants all the time, but that single year changed me as a fangirl. My challenge showed me that being a little crazy and aiming for self-improvement weren't contradictory at all.

This might sound like a silly story to you. I know that the fangirl rep suffers some damage when we focus on elements of a more superficial nature, like fashion or hair. But show me anyone who doesn't think attractiveness is an element in girl crushing or shipping, and I will show you someone who has never seen really good hairporn. It's as if she lived in an alternate universe where Connie Britton doesn't exist.

If you've gotten this far into the book and don't know what hairporn is, then let me enlighten you. It can be a scary word to people who don't speak fandom. Hairporn is just a word for the common fangirl love for an actress's really pretty, creys-inducing hair. It's hair styled with the rarest of unicorn tears; the kind of shampoo commercial locks to which we all aspire. Fandoms rise and fall on a sea of good hair and varying styles. One day I will host a game show where contestants have to guess the season of a TV show by the female characters' hair. Don't tell me you wouldn't watch the hell out of that.

But hairporn is more than just a fun beauty obsession; it's more of a metaphor for how to live your life. There is a difference between finding creative ways to feel confident about your appearance and wasting your emotional energy and bank account on the unattainable. Because on top of all the glam, there is also The Glare, that ineffable something that helps a character radiate the confidence we wish we could summon for ourselves. So to follow the Hairporn Way, we'll need to accomplish several tasks in this chapter. One is to debunk societal and media narratives about beauty. Another is to summon the courage to ask for help when you need it. Finally, we'll talk about how you can practice your power poses and conquer like a BAMF. But first, let's clear out the smoke and take down the mirrors we use to compare ourselves to our favorite actresses.

It's a Wig!

When you choose to set new goals for your appearance, fictional folks and celebrities can be the inspiration, but they can't be the yardstick. There is no exercise routine, no special cleanse, and no "what's in my makeup bag" reveal that is going to give you an instant romantic comedy makeover. Unlike fiction, you can't teach yourself a new skill or get in shape in the course of a thirty-second Katy Perry–accompanied montage. When your goal is to look and feel powerful and beautiful, the game is completely different.

In case you're not convinced, here are a few things that your favorite actresses have (on *and* off set) that you don't.

- **AN ARMY!** You do not have a hair and makeup team on standby.

- **FREE STUFF!** Many actresses can get their hair and makeup done for free just so the stylist can brag. They can also walk off the set with their character's wardrobe.

- **TIME!** I don't know about you, but I don't have hours to spend in make-it-work mode.

To keep my feet on the ground, I like to save pictures of celebrities in casual mode on my phone to remind me that not everyone always looks like they've had a three-hour prep. And by casual, no I don't mean Taylor Swift trotting out of her New York fortress in a jaunty little hat. That's just wizardry. I'm talking about actresses with no makeup, dumb hair clips, and mismatched clothing and ugly boots. They're not perfect, so why are you trying so hard to be?

If this tactic doesn't work, I'm going to teach you an important mantra that you can chant when you start comparing yourself. So repeat after me: IT'S.A.WIG. This is a phrase I use again and again to remind myself that a lot of what we see on television or in movies isn't real. Wigs and hair extensions are used by way more celebrities than you think (a classic example is Julianna Margulies on *The Good Wife*—that amazingly shiny straight hair is not sprouting from her head!) and it's important that we take this real hair mythology and bring it out into the light of day and expose it for what it really is.

My Body Is Ready

Fangirls stare at women a whole freaking lot. We cry, we analyze, we reblog, we rank, and we copycat. So when our beauty standard becomes actresses whose job it is to look fabulous, we put ourselves at risk for having issues with our body image. Research shows that approximately 75 percent of women who are categorized as average weight think negatively about their appearance quite frequently. The more you think about your body, the worse you tend to feel about it. When you see Black Widow kicking butt in her skintight outfit, you may be staring down at your tummy and despairing that you'll never look like that. There are a lot of risk factors for this type of unhealthy focus, but here are a few that the fangirl may encounter.

- Hearing frequent negative or positive comments about women's bodies from others

- Exposing oneself often to idealized body types

- Experiencing discrimination based on race, sexual orientation, gender identity, etc.

It is really fun to cry about beautiful ladies. But when you see tweet after tweet of "Kerry Washington is so beautiful I want to die," a certain feeling of inferiority starts to become ingrained. Because we watch so much TV, we experience a high exposure to idealized body types. I turn on the TV, and it tells me that beautiful women are tall and thin but miraculously have big boobs. Even though we know that it is medically impossible for many women to have so little body fat and not have her lady parts shut down due to hormone imbalance, we still buy into the idea, don't we?

Women (and many men) use their hypernegative focus on their bodies to project what's going on inside their brain. You might not be able to fix family drama, your bank account, or feelings of anxiety or depression, but you can lose weight by exercising like a maniac or starving yourself. This intense focus on your body might make you feel like you have control over your life, when in reality you're just creating more challenges for yourself. Eating healthy and exercising are important parts of good mental health, but not when they're just distractions from getting the additional help you need.

You might be thinking, *isn't complaining about my thighs a constitutional right?* We all do it, and it can even be a bonding topic between fangirls. But if you want to travel farther on the road to becoming a BAMF, that means taking responsibility for how you challenge the narratives you absorb from real life and fiction. Ways to do this are

- Being intentional about noticing nonphysical traits

- Highlighting women who don't embody physical ideals

- Avoiding words like *perfect* and *flawless*

- Eschewing "Who wore it best?" comparison games

- Abstaining from media that promotes unhealthy ideals

- Promoting media that encourages hiring diverse women

If you watch predominantly American shows or movies, your eyes are bombarded with celebrities and models who look perfect. If you need inspiration for challenging this narrative, then I would encourage you to look to the British. Because TV in the UK has done what American TV could never do—prove that you can still love and admire ordinary looking people on your TV screen. The British teach us that aging isn't something to fear, that wrinkles are beautiful, and that women can wear a wide range of sizes and still be fabulous. So let's raise our reading glasses to more elderly lesbian make-outs on *Broadchurch*, more Violet Crawley schooling the crap out of everyone on *Downton Abbey*, and more of *Doctor Who*'s Prime Minister Harriet Jones saving the planet.

American media also perpetuate some damaging narratives. Media tells us that beautiful women are predominantly white, thin, and younger than their male counterparts. If you're not a person of color, then you may not realize that you have the privilege of seeing people who look like you all the time in TV and movies. If you're a minority, you have to search harder to find these role models. As a fangirl, it is your responsibility to think about how your viewing choices impact the demand for diverse women in media. As I was writing this book, I had to examine my own biases toward continuously referencing certain actresses. So think about what you can do to support the belief that there are all kinds of beauty, and all kinds of heroes, and that fiction should celebrate that diversity.

Project ZOMG

So now that you've thought about how to shake off some of the stereotypes of beauty, let's talk about how you assemble a fashion squad to help you achieve a look that makes you feel amazing. Remember, the fanwoman life is about how you feel and not about what other people think. To quote Miss Phryne Fisher, "A woman should dress first and foremost for her own pleasure." Asking for help can be the hardest task when it comes to your appearance. I don't hesitate for a second if I can't figure out how to learn new software on my computer or assemble a piece of furniture, but for some reason asking a makeup counter lady for her opinion is like opening my soul to the harsh light of day. Suddenly I'm lurching through Sephora like Gollum on his way to Mordor.

There's this assumption that women are supposed to magically have all this aesthetic knowledge, regardless of whether you've been taught or whether you're even interested in it. Never assume that you can't ask for help because you've reached a certain age. When you ask for professional help, you're giving someone an opportunity to share his or her gift. Why would you deny a person that opportunity? They won't think you're weird, and if you ask a dumb question, they're a stranger, so who cares? If you've done what I suggested earlier and kept an eye out for celebrities in their natural states (celebrity Instagram accounts are often great for this, as many seem more willing to post casual images there) then you've seen that your favorite actress, when left to her own devices, doesn't live as if she's always on a red carpet, so you shouldn't feel ashamed because you have to assemble your own hairporn and wardrobe team.

Your own squad doesn't have to be an army of paid professionals either. Your fandom can be your friends here, too. Ask your fellow fangirl to teach you how to pincurl your hair like Agent Carter, how to dress for less like Aria Montgomery, or to design a sweet Ruby Rose–inspired tattoo for you. You might find that you'll make someone's day by asking for their help. You don't have to add me to that list, but I want to share with you what knowledge I do have about snagging inspiration and authentic pieces from the fictional greats. My hair intelligence isn't too high, but I can teach you a thing or two about what we call the Fashion ID. As the great Regina George once said, "Get in loser, we're going shopping."

The Most Dangerous Game

To begin, I think it's also important to distinguish between inspiration and copy-cattery when it comes to hair and wardrobe choices. When I was knee-deep in the Emma Pillsbury wardrobe scavenger hunt, I found myself buying clothes that didn't even look good on me just because I could find the exact item worn on the show. I had transformed into Captain Ahab, consumed by my search for the great white eyelet jacket. Finding an exact match is a dopamine rush for sure, but 99.9 percent of the population isn't going to notice that you're wearing the dress from last week's episode of your favorite show. But sometimes we see a dress on *The Mindy Project*, and we simply must find The Precious. So let me be your Jedi wardrobe master and show you the ways of the Internet fashion hunt.

STEP 1. TWEET. It is very rare for a show's wardrobe guru to not be on social media. So before you go trolling fashion databases into the wee hours of the night, Google the show's name and the phrase "costume designer," and you can easily find their Twitter account. Very kindly (aka without weird fangirl words), ask them what your favorite character was wearing. Be specific, attach a photo, and try to keep it recent. If you're asking from three seasons ago, it might be difficult for him or her to recall. Remember, the costume designer wants the work to be recognized, and designers want them to sell the clothes, so you're not annoying anyone. If you don't get a response after a second tweet, however, I wouldn't press. Move on to step 2.

STEP 2. ASK THE INTERNET. A lot of times finding your answer is as simple as Googling the outfit description or posting a text query on Tumblr. You will find folks who are similarly interested and can share intel with you. Sites like wornontv.net and apps like Spylight can give great overviews of fashion matches very quickly after an episode. If those attempts don't work, your next stop should be ShopStyle.com. Describe the clothing you're looking for, and check the color and style, and suddenly you have every blue sheath dress currently being sold right in front of you. Yes, it will take a while to sort through pages of matches, so the more specific you can be the better, but it's worth it if it's something you simply must have. Also if you can't afford the actual item (like Olivia Pope's $3,000 Burberry trench coat), ShopStyle is great for finding look

alikes. You can type in the description and narrow the price range, and you'll be thrilled with what you can find.

STEP 3. EBAY. If you can't find it on the Internet, eBay is your next stop to search. eBay is like the Mos Eisley space port—you will never find a more wretched hive of junk, but occasionally great legends will pass through that you don't want to miss. Because TV shows shoot months ahead of when you watch an episode, you may also find that the item is no longer being sold. But don't panic! Create an eBay account and then save a search with the designer name, clothing description, and your approximate size. Be specific or you're going to get a lot of bad matches in your inbox (these are not the droids you're looking for). It might take months, but one day the match will come. I still occasionally get an email with matches from *Glee* clothes I no longer care about. A long wait will also ensure that you really want the item, so it's wise to use the twenty-four-hour rule. If you still want it after twenty-four hours and can afford the piece, then it's safe to go ahead. But beware of Buy-It-Now options that tempt your clicky finger.

Finally, if you're content with your wardrobe and just want to play dress up, or you're not sure whether to purchase something, there is no greater site than polyvore.com. It's a free alternative to playing dress up at the mall or accidentally buying stuff you don't want or need. On polyvore you can search the piece you want, and create clothing sets with other items. Create a new look inspired by your favorite TV lady. Pair an item with other clothing you own to see whether it fits into your wardrobe.

So enjoy the hunt! Be savvy and be smart, but above all be consumed by the love of the game more than the love of material possessions. You don't have to spend any money at all to feel BAMFy, so let's take a look at the cheapest and most effective way to live a life full of hairporn. It's something we call the power pose.

Power Poses Revamped

So now maybe you have a few ideas of who to recruit for a hair transformation and where to start searching for fictional fashion on the Internet. While your appearance is a huge part of developing your self-confidence, that doesn't mean the right clothes and hair can summon that BAMF courage. Perhaps the most essential piece of The Glare is the power pose. Your body language has an impact on your brain and your personality, and it impacts how other people treat and respect you.

Amy Cuddy, a professor at Harvard Business School, did a TED talk a few years ago in which she argues that if you can "make yourself big" before a test or a big meeting, you'll be more courageous, less anxious, and act like a leader. And she has the science to back it up. A study tested participants who spent a few minutes with their feet propped up on a desk with their fingers laced behind their heads, and they found that this power pose lifted testosterone levels by 20 percent and decreased cortisol levels (a stress hormone) by 25 percent.

Where do I sign up, right? This is a no-brainer, a low-energy task that has instant results. So why am I not standing up with my hands on my hips and my legs wide apart (aka the Wonder Woman) more often? Probably because I'm hunched over my iPhone or splayed over the couch like a dead animal while I watch HBO. Cuddy's recommendations are fantastic, but let me introduce a few more moves that I have noticed from years of ~~careful research~~ TV viewing. Unlike Cuddy, we don't have science per se to back these up, but we do have screencaps of Tatiana Maslany looking intimidating as hell. That'll do.

THE COMMANDER. Stand at the head of a conference room table or your desk for this power play. To huddle your troops, place both palms flat on the table, and lean forward. Be sure to make eye contact with your target, and then say what you mean like you mean it. Don't preface your sentences with "I don't know but" or end with an apology. *You know what you are talking about, and you're not sorry.*

THE BAMF LEAN. Leaders use this move when they want to enlighten hapless colleagues. It is perhaps the trademark move of badass TV ladies, and you can practice at home with any tall chair. Stand behind the chair and place your elbows on top. Lean forward and lace your fingers together. Some sort of bling like a necklace or fancy watch helps the overall effect. But above all, you need glasses. You should be wearing them (for the intimidating over-the-glasses "Did you just say that" peer) or dangling them from your fingers.

THE ONE-ARM. I've seen this pose on *How to Get Away with Murder* a lot. This move highlights your fancy clothes and exudes gazelle-like prowess as you stand at the front of a classroom or a conference room. Standing up and facing the room, you should have a table, desk, or tall chair next to you. Place one hand on top of the table, and place the other hand on your hip. To quote *Veep*'s Selina Meyer while she pulls off this move, "I'm going to completely obliterate him with my poise and sophistication." That pretty much sums it up.

THE MERKEL. I don't know how many pictures you've seen of German Chancellor Angela Merkel, but 95 percent of the time she is shoving her hand in a dude's face to emphasize how wrong he is. There are variations, from the palm open approach to the accusatory finger point. Add a look of disgust for the full effect. If she could do it to Putin and David Cameron, then you can pull it off with that pseudo-intellectual dude bro in your class who is full of himself.

THE COUCH ARM. Of all power poses, there is one move to rule them all. The Couch Arm is more a way of life than an actual pose. To copy Diane Lockhart's signature move from *The Good Wife*, sit on the far side of a couch, draping your arm across the back. Cross your legs, tilt your head back, maybe cackle a little, and enjoy your reign.

To get started, you can try out a few poses or come up with your own. The power pose isn't about being attractive or seductive. It's about building confidence and decreasing stress enough to say what you think and do what needs to be done. Remember, it's not about how you look, but how you'll feel as you conquer.

So there you have it. The secret to feeling fabulous is to check your standards, ask for help, and literally, lean in. If you take any piece of understanding away from this chapter, aside from the glory of the Merkel, I want it to be the knowledge that self-confidence is not something you have to earn or deserve.

My first TV fashion hero wasn't a woman who had a fancy luncheon or a club opening to dress for every day (sorry, Carrie Bradshaw). Emma Pillsbury was someone who made the effort when maybe the only comment she'll get is an insult. So we should all be so brave and stop waiting for that imaginary occasion when wearing the clothes or walking the walk is what *makes* the day special. A life full of hairporn isn't a life full of hairspray or extensions. It's a life where your look and your confidence communicate to the world that something season finale–worthy is about to happen.

To boost your confidence, I want you to do one thing for me. I want you to pick a day this week, and take that item— that skirt, your fancy pants, that piece of jewelry, or bowtie or pair of shoes that you've been saving for the day that Oprah calls you up to tell you you're on her new favorite things list— and wear it. Crank it up a notch! Then go somewhere. Make your significant other take you out. Go out to eat with friends. Have a classy Downton-esque dinner, only without the passive aggressive banter. Just be fabulous regardless of who notices, and see what happens. While you're conquering, you can try these exercises as well.

BLAZE IT! If you know you'd like to glam it up a bit, and you're not sure where to start, then I suggest you make a list of all the fashion feats that you'd like to try even though they scare the crap out of you. Maybe you've never tried wearing red lipstick, because you're afraid it won't work on you. Or maybe those shoes or that dress seem a little bit too risky. Give yourself permission to make as many fashion mistakes as you can in a single week. Don't worry if you wear a blazer to school and people ask you why you're so dressed up. Sometimes you just gotta blaze it!

WARDROBE CHECK. Find a fangirl friend you trust, and tell her who your fashion icon is, real or fictional. Make sure she has a sense of this person's style, and then let her loose. For a day, a week, as long as you want, anything she picks from your closet you are required to wear. Pretend that you're an actress and you don't have much say in the matter. Listen to your wardrobe stylist, and do what she says. For more fun, go shopping with her and try on whatever she suggests. You don't have to buy anything to get inspired to start channeling your muse.

CHAPTER 5
FACT OR FAN FICTION

> The other day I started a 65k word crossover fic for two characters from shows I've never even watched.
>
> **—ELLY, TWENTY-TWO**

> You join chat rooms, you write poetry, you post Doogie Howser fanfic. It's all normal, right?
>
> **—WILLOW, *BUFFY THE VAMPIRE SLAYER***

Writing is one of my many day jobs. I write about mental illness and the future of psychotherapy. I write about technology and how it influences our relationships. I write this very sentence in a book about being a fangirl. But I have a secret—I also write about two imaginary people who really want to kiss each other. Yes, I said it. I write fan fiction. But you can't hurt me world, because right now, in my mind, I am landing on a metaphorical aircraft carrier. Triumphantly flapping in the breeze behind me, a giant banner reads, MISSION ACCOMPLISHED. NO SHAME.

I won't lie. It took me years to pick up and carry that banner. Years of squawking like a bird when somebody looked over my shoulder and asked me what I was typing so furiously on my laptop. I would tilt my smartphone just a leeeeetle bit to the right so no one could see on the bus. I would laugh along with others who made fun of fan fiction while I was crying unicorn tears on the inside. But one day, I finally figured out that there is no shame in fiction, fan or not.

When you're introduced to someone who writes fan fiction, you've just met a person who uses her imagination about a hundred times more than the majority of the adult population. If you write fic, you're not afraid to lose yourself in other worlds. Rather, you dive headfirst into them. You know that fictional characters don't disappear when the credits roll. They aren't meant to be boxed and preserved airtight on the shelf—they're supposed to be taken down and spun around until someone's head pops off. When you're writing fan fiction, you're pulling the dolls and action figures from under your bed. You dust off the characters, put them in a room together, and see what happens. Being an adult doesn't negate the necessity of that playtime. It fuels you and keeps your brain active. Those butterflies in your stomach poke their heads out of their cocoons when your favorite romantic pairing is nervous around each other. Your palms latch onto your cheeks when they begin to flirt. Your mom may not be calling for you to clean your room, but you still have to snap back into reality at inconvenient moments. But the stories will still be there when you need them.

Fan fiction is as old as story. The Internet has certainly aided the expansion of the art form, but humans have craved it since they started painting leaping antelopes on their living room cave walls. The creation stories in the Bible were borrowed from more ancient peoples, and who's to say that hieroglyphics aren't actually multichapter slash fic? If Shakespeare were posting *Richard III* or *Henry V* on fanfic.net, he'd have "these characters are not mine" posted as a disclaimer. If you count historical fiction like Michael Shaara's *The Killer Angels*, a reimagining of the battle of Gettysburg, then technically fan fiction has won a Pulitzer Prize.

I could go on and cite modern authors who've gotten their start writing fan fiction or by readapting stories like *Wicked*. We could spend a lot of time reviewing the history and culture of fan fiction, but I want to talk about how you can use your fic-writing muscle to break down walls and fears. In this chapter, you'll also learn about the many benefits of reading fiction, and I'll talk about how to begin to workshop your own life story. Together, we'll explore what it takes to start developing solid and intriguing plot points for your life. So just for a little while, let me be the beta for your new narrative. Ready to dive in?

Why Write Fic?

Like other fangirl qualities, society teaches us to wear our fanfic appetite like a badge of shame. Fan fiction is frequently the butt of standup jokes or the hobby of the weirdo on a television show. Everyone daydreams, yet we are supposed to be embarrassed for rubbing chalk over our imaginations until those stories are captured on paper. What they call embarrassing, I see as courageous. Because the fangirl doesn't want to live a life where she watches a movie or reads a book and never imagines what happens off-camera or off-page. When I asked my friend Camilla, the amazing artist for this book, why she cared about fan fiction, she said it best:

> I want to know these characters in those time lapses, and their inner thoughts during scenes. The spin their lives would take if they were in 1920 Ireland or in a zombie apocalypse or if they woke up in another body. But most of all I want to see them be true to themselves even then, because that's why I fell in love with them in the first place.

For the fangirl, the hobby often serves two purposes. The first is a healthy vacation from day-to-day life that jump-starts the imagination. Pure, squee-worthy fun. Sometimes people have a hard time justifying work that has no reward other than bringing joy to others and themselves. That joy can be a huge payoff, because a really good fic writer is a god in the world of fandom. She sculpts from the clay of an old story and breathes new life into it. So much life that the characters virtually stand up and run away from her, rebelling and doing whatever they damn well please. It is incredibly human to feel the primal instinct to take a story and start weaving another layer. In fact, I would argue that it is one of the most human of characteristics.

Have you ever written fan fiction?

YEP 69.4%

NOPE 30.6%

Second, fic writing serves as a kind of training ground for people who want to be writers.

Websites like Fanfiction.net and Archive of Our Own are sort of battle rooms a la *Ender's Game*. You can't fight aliens until you float around in zero G for a bit first. Similarly, NASA doesn't want to shoot astronauts into space before they bob around in swimming pools or crash a few times via a flight simulator. In the same way, fanfic writers play around with dialogue and plot construction in a safe environment. You'd think that there would be a lot of pressure to write scenes for characters who usually spit words written by screenwriters who make millions of dollars. But in truth it is much safer, as you already know that the characters are beloved by fans who are eager for more of their stories. Because of this unquenchable thirst, you're more likely to get positive feedback from readers, which can build confidence. So it's a win-win for both.

To the novice writer, making the jump to creating your own characters can seem as ominous as the frigid blackness of space. In case you can't tell, the point I'm trying to make here is that I just really like space analogies. Maybe you're one of those fic writers who'd like to make the leap from borrowing characters to molding your own. Rainbow Rowell's novel *Fangirl* is an excellent story of how an innocent endeavor can evolve into a mechanism for avoiding the real world. Like her protagonist, Cath, maybe you find yourself hesitant to climb out of the fic flight simulator and launch into orbit. It's normal to want to feel the ground below you. You fear rejection, and you assume the worst when you don't receive immediate positive feedback.

Maybe you're a person who is content to write fic and nothing else. Even if you have the talent, you don't necessarily want to be a writer, and that's okay! Every fangirl, however, has some sort of dream that she wants to move from the test lab to the launchpad (last one, I promise!). Everyone has her own story to write, so how do you challenge yourself? How do you keep from being too comfortable with what feels safe? Let's dig in.

Imaginative Adulting

Good news! The very same skills you use to write fic are the ones that you need to do some extreme adulting. We've gathered some pretty handy tools so far in our story. You have some science/knowledge about how your brain works and a good code to live by thanks to the female powerhouses in fiction. But now you need to kick-start the vehicle that can actually take you from point A to point Adult: your imagination. Even if you're a fangirl, part of becoming an adult includes sometimes setting aside random whims of fantasy and focusing on the task ahead. I like to think of it as a sort of un-Peter-Panning of yourself. Who has time for nonsense when there's a job to be done? *random adult grumbles* But that doesn't mean you let your imaginative muscles atrophy.

To really get what I'm saying, I'd like for you to take a minute and think about what would happen if a five-year-old showed up with a tiny briefcase at any adult job. How would she operate differently in that environment? Perhaps she'd have impromptu dance parties in the conference room. Maybe she'd suggest Laser Dragons as a reasonable solution to defeating your competitors. There'd probably be a lot more naps, and who needs HR when you can hire an imaginary friend, right? At first glance, hiring a tiny human would be an absolute disaster. But if you look closely, you'll find that there is some wisdom to the five-year-old way of life.

Transitioning to adulthood isn't just about increasing your knowledge. We are also taught to alter our behaviors. Suddenly we look at the crowd, and we become self-conscious if we deviate from the course set out for us. You probably care a lot more about what other people think than a five-year-old does, so that's why you don't burst into tears and flop about on the floor in the middle of a big meeting. While this is an important skill, sometimes we begin to filter our words and actions too much based on what the group says. We shy away from challenges or thinking outside the box. "What will people say?" is a question I ask myself way more often than I should.

Yes, the fangirl has an extraordinary capacity for preserving her imagination and carrying it with her into adulthood. But while we can find a hundred AU ideas for a ship, sometimes we struggle to translate our imaginative abilities into our day-to-day lives. Basically, we struggle to live our destiny as divergent adults. Divergent is more than a famous young adult series; it's a way of being. It means deviating from a prearranged course. Let me give you an example—have you heard about the test where they give a paperclip to a kindergartener and an adult? When you ask the kindergartener how many different things you can do with the paperclip, she can generate hundreds of answers. But when you ask the adult, she struggles to think of more than five. Because at some point in our educational history, we rolled over and just started accepting what we were taught. We flipped to the back of the book for the answer rather than generating our own solutions.

Becoming a fanwoman is about training your brain to see points in your life like a kindergartener sees a paperclip. Obstacles aren't necessarily obstacles when you see them as challenges. Suddenly a tragedy is turned into a comedy. An episode of *Mad Men* is now a motivator for your work, or a kick-ass Joan Holloway quote is your fuel for taking a risk. Life is not a video game where you pick up certain tools that serve only a single function. What distracts you from your worries can be what encourages you to be brave, and that imagination you use to pair two imaginary people together can be the same imagination that makes a kick-ass presentation in class or a great pitch to your boss.

When it comes to your imagination, you can use it or you can lose it. When you limit those powers you have to a fandom or the Internet, then you're missing out on a great story. So how do you hot-wire your imagination? You start by exploring new territories outside of your favorite fanfic author. One of the ways to do this is to fall in love with a great book.

A Novel Power

While they're both central to the experience of the fangirl, reading and watching a screen are two very different actions. "We perform a book, and we attend the performance," writes Peter Mendelsund, author of *What We See When We Read*. "As readers, we are both the conductor and the orchestra, as well as the audience." Mendelsund argues that reading requires much more of our imagination because it is not a linear process. We have to imagine what characters look like with an incomplete description, and we have to consider what might happen to them long before we reach the page of reckoning. We're stage managing and directing and adding a touch of makeup to the cast, feats that are diminished, Mendelsund argues, when we headcast our favorite actors or project familiar movie sets onto a novel. Whoops!

What does this mean, besides the fact that I am incredibly upset that Oscar-winner Julianne Moore can't star in my books? It means that as a reading adult, your imagination is riper than the child who relies on the picture book. Mentally assembling the hints an author gives us is perhaps the best exercise there is to keep our imaginations buff and ready to conquer. Of course there are many other benefits to diving into a novel. Bookworms get tossed all sorts of labels in today's world, both positive and negative. But neuroscientists and psychologists are just starting to research the impact of fiction on the mind, and what they're finding is rather exciting. We all know that retreating into the depths of a novel is a well-applauded act of self-care. It's certainly better than microwaving nachos for a marathon of Kardashian antics. But it's now arguable that reading fiction can actually make you a better person.

Psychologists say that reading fiction on a regular basis better equips you to understand and empathize with others. Even when you control for variables like gender, age, and personality, there's still a relationship between fiction reading and empathy. How does this work exactly? To start, your brain doesn't register much of a difference between a real-life experience and events in a story. If you read the phrase *leathery scent* in a Destiel fic, both the language processing and the olfactory parts of your brain light up. A descriptive narrative is neurologically transportive. So while you might not actually be kilting it up in 1743 Scotland when you're reading *Outlander*, your brain says you are. Hawt.

In addition to activating parts of our brain associated with smells, touches, and body movement, fiction also allows us to enter into another person's thoughts and emotions. For the reader, it is a safe way to practice understanding others who might have different values or beliefs from ours. We're teaching ourselves multicultural empathy as we see commonalities in the human experience and also the differences between our lives and others. Now don't get me wrong. Developing real understanding requires throwing yourself into real-life scenarios and relationships, not making assumptions based on one fictional person's experience. But reading fiction is sort of a boot camp for the understanding skills that build a more compassionate human. In short, you're less likely to engage in nastiness.

In addition to the empathy discovery, psychological research about fiction completely debunks the myth of the antisocial bookworm. Compared to nonfiction readers, fiction folks are less lonely, less stressed, and have larger social networks. So if you're a college or graduate student buried in academic texts, it might be worth the effort to be brave and cross the Narrow Sea toward a little fiction reading.

So here's what we know. Reading novels:

- Strengthens divergent thinking

- Increases empathetic understanding

- Transports your brain to the action

- Indicates you might be more social and less stressed

It's important I mimic your statistics teacher here and remind you that correlation is not causation. It's going to take a lot more time and research to unlock the effects of fiction. But the research does show that reading novels explains a little bit beyond what our personalities or gender tell us about the ability to empathize. That fiction is a teleportation device to infinite worlds and infinite minds. So honestly, any thinking human being would want to be all over that.

So given this logic, every fangirl should be the most compassionate human you've ever met, right? Hahahahahahahaha. Sorry, I just needed a second.

Reading different types of fan fiction is absolutely a way to expand your thinking and challenge your values. The catch is that if you're reading about characters who look, think, and act in only a certain way, then you're not engaging in true imaginative and empathetic exercise. If you're reading fan fiction about only the same two characters in multiple AU settings or about the stereotypical white female teenager in a postapocalyptic scenario, then you'll get stuck. Your brain won't benefit. It'll feel that dopamine for sure, but the experience is anything but transportive.

So how do you escape that repetitive neurological commute, and shift your mind off of autopilot? You must diversify. Introduce yourself to authors and characters with different ages, races, nationalities, sexual orientations, abilities, and religions from your own. Start a book club with friends to discuss your thoughts. You might be surprised by how fascinating the larger world is compared to the small, safe ones we sometimes carve out for ourselves. The more curious you are about the diversity of the human experience, the more you also expand your own narrative.

Finding Your Own Narrative

At this point you're probably thinking, wow, if only there were a type of therapy that appealed to my love of fan fiction. Ahh, but wait! You can take the ideas I've introduced so far and run with them, or you can take a look and see what's behind Door Number 2. Which is a lovely mode of thinking called narrative therapy.

History scholars accept that there is more than one way to interpret an event. The problem is that we still live in societies that want to tell us what our story is. This is how privilege and oppression are perpetuated across centuries, but on a smaller scale, it also influences how we feel about ourselves. There are dominant narratives in society about your body, your accomplishments, your personality, your race and ethnicity, your gender and your sexuality. Even about being a fangirl.

If this sounds limiting, that's because it is. Think of all the stories that movies tell us about how women should look and act. These expectations are literally impossible to reconcile because they are constantly contradicting one another. If you subscribe to that story, then every time you do something considered "inappropriate," like eat a cookie or stand up to a coworker, you are basically screwed. Narrative therapists believe that problems happen in our lives when we internalize these self-defeating views. We start telling ourselves stories that don't have to be true. This is where our old buddy Carl from Chapter 1 comes in. He starts reading the same old script that we've been spoon-fed by the world around us, and we feel as doomed as a female character on *Supernatural*.

How do we get unstuck? By constructing our own stories about ourselves, and by calling a problem what it is. By being divergent. You don't have to give your problem a human name like Carl. Maybe you call it Insecurity or Fear or Procrastination. Narrative therapists encourage their clients to talk about the problem like it's outside themselves. So rather than asking, "When did you feel afraid?" they might ask, "When did Fear get the best of you? When did Fear convince you not to apply for the job? When did Fear crash through your roof and ninja kick you in the face?"

Once you start viewing the problem as outside yourself, you can start pinpointing moments when you won the battle. When you resisted the story that you are weak, or boring, or lazy, and you behaved in a way that changes that original narrative. Using these exceptions, you can start weaving a new story for yourself that's a much more optimistic one. You don't have to look far to see this process happening in fiction all the time. Joss Whedon wanted to debunk the blond girl horror victim narrative when he created *Buffy*. Shonda Rhimes rejected the narrative that an African American female can't be a smart and powerful protagonist in *Scandal* and *How to Get Away with Murder*. *Orange Is the New Black* challenged transphobic and homophobic narratives as well as many about criminality.

I could go on and on, but the basic idea is that when it leans toward self-improvement, really good character development is all about rejecting the narratives we inherit and replacing them with our own. *Lost* is a brilliant example of this concept, with the crash of Oceanic Flight 815 moving character development into hyperdrive. Think of the narratives that the characters once accepted about themselves and the problems they caused. John Locke was the disabled man who would never be a leader. Charlie was the junkie rock star. Sawyer was a selfish conman. Kate was a murderer. Sayid was a torturer. In the plot, problems usually arise when the characters fall back into what these assigned stories say about how they should behave. Being on the island was a means of wiping these narratives off the map, literally and figuratively, so that each character could construct a new story. Lucky for us, we don't have to crash on a freaky island to ignite this type of character development. You can start looking for small ways to retell how you live your life. Here's how.

#PlotDevelopment

Fanfic writers love to throw their characters into uncomfortable situations that make them grow as individuals. They play god because they know that it will benefit them in the long run, that those challenges will launch them into a career or a relationship that is worth the struggle. And these are the characters that usually appeal to us as fangirls. So why don't you follow their examples? Why do you bemoan stories that lack good character development, but are perfectly content with the status quo in your own life? Nobody wants to read a story in which the main character gets up and sleepwalks her way through the same routine every day. We read and write stories about people who are put in impossible situations and rise above them. So why should your life be any different? A truly motivated fangirl isn't living her life for the reviews, for the praise and approval of other people. She is living her life the way she wants her story to be told.

This frame of reference is relevant whether you want to be a writer or not. And like any real change, it's hella difficult. As Jillian Michaels yells at me in her exercise videos, "Get comfortable with being uncomfortable!" There is a trick you can use to motivate yourself, and that's to reframe the challenges of your life as plot development. When you show up to a dance class for the first time. When you ask your crush out on a date. When you apply for the impossible job. Just tell yourself, "Whatever happens, this is plot development." Dumped by your girlfriend? PLOT DEVELOPMENT. Have a cranky boss at work? PLOT DEVELOPMENT! Crapped on by a pigeon . . . probably bad luck. When the action rises in fiction, you don't throw your phone across the room. You perk up and pay attention. Real life shouldn't be any different.

You are your author, your protagonist, and your audience. The more you push yourself forward, the more you push your story forward. And like reading, this process is never linear. We're given imperfect information and the future looks blurry, but we stick with the story because we choose to trust in where it's headed.

So let's say that your goal is to be a writer. Every morning you get up, and you stare at the blinking cursor for ten minutes, check Twitter six times, and say "Screw it, I'm going to law school." We've all been there. Instead, put your fingers on the keyboard and say, "This is the part of my story where the protagonist tries really hard and maybe fails. But she gets up and tries again. She types a bad sentence. She tries another, because she doesn't let Fear crash through her ceiling and hold her hostage. This is exactly what makes her appealing to the reader."

Yes, there are those people who write the perfect first drafts or nail their first job interview out of college. But you and I are not those people, and neither are your favorite characters. How many times have they gotten pushed down? How many times have *you* pushed them down in your own writing? That's the thing about being a survivor: you have to encounter obstacles that require surviving. As writers and readers, we know these truths backward and forward. But as humans who bumble about, having to worrying about paying taxes and getting our teeth cleaned, we suffer from constant amnesia when it comes to this basic truth—that a story gets worse before it gets better and that things always look like they're going to hell in the beginning. Also, we know that intermissions are for stretching your legs and eating a cookie before you return to the story. So feel free to take a quick break before you try out these exercises I recommend.

HAVE AN AU DAY. In fan fiction, *AU* is an acronym for "alternate universe." Already existing characters are moved into different worlds, genres, time periods, or jobs. While we're given only one life and the present, that doesn't mean that we can't shake things up. Have an alternate universe day to inspire you to greatness. Maybe you dress up like your favorite BAMFy lady or take a day trip to an unfamiliar place. You don't have to stop playing pretend just because you're an adult. An AU day might mean role-playing with your significant other or having lunch with a friend and pretending you have totally different careers.

STORY ARC. If you have a daunting task ahead of you, consider mapping out a story arc like you would for a fic. Labeling conflict as a part of the story where the heroine faces her fears and conquers them (rather than dives into a tailspin) can be incredibly helpful. If you were paying attention to your literature teachers in school, you know that most stories have five parts: exposition, rising action, climax, falling action, and resolution. Say that you're studying for finals and you start to feel the terror of failure creep up into your throat. Map out how you want the story to progress. Your commitment to studying is the rising action. Showing up with your game face on test day is the climax. But then you flip to the first page of the test, and the action begins to drive toward resolution. YOU'VE TOTALLY GOT THIS.

CASTING DIRECTOR. When you decide to write a story, you have to decide who's worthy of including in your cast of characters. Who's a great character in your real life that inspires you? If you haven't seen her in a while, invite her to lunch. If your story is missing a good friend who pulls you out of your Netflix hibernation, then go find one. If your tale needs a lady mentor worth swooning over, then start holding auditions. If your story is in need of a love interest (no, celebrities and fictional people don't count), then it's time for a meet-cute (or just a meet in general). You never know when someone else will want to cast you in his or her own life.

If these exercises sound like a lot of work, that's because they are. The reality is that working on a new chapter for your own life is even more rewarding than putting two love-struck fictional idiots in a room and seeing what happens. Fangirling is where your story begins, not where it ends. So as our story continues, let's take a look at another of the favorite pastimes of the fangirl. Grab your lifejacket and your feelings, because we're headed out into open water.

CHAPTER 6
GOING DOWN WITH THE SHIP

So I just watched the first episode of *The X-Files*. It took me seven minutes to start shipping Scully and Mulder.

—KEARSIE, TWENTY-THREE

To me, our relationship makes perfect sense. You want me to propose to you, I propose to you. You say no, I say fine, I never wanna see you again. You drive me nuts telling me you want me to propose again, I do, you turn me down. Next thing I know I'm in a court of law where I've got to propose to you or go to jail. It's the classic American love story.

—SAM MALONE, *CHEERS*

Shipping wars

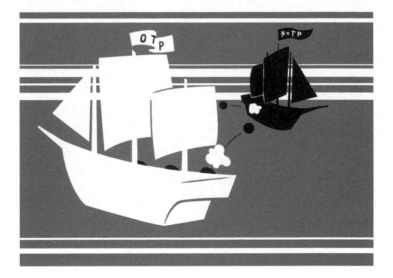

The fangirl is no landlubber. She is at home out on the open ocean air, the salty spray blowing across her face as she leans over the bow of her vessel. She is the master and commander of her own journey, but that doesn't mean she won't be tossed about in choppy waters or have plot-size cannonballs hurled in her general direction on more than one occasion. If you want to be a fangirl, you have to be seaworthy. The view from the shore may seem safe and scenic at first, but sooner or later the boat you were meant to board will dock and call you forth on some great adventure.

Yes nerds, I'm talking about ships. From where does the term originate? It's claimed by the *X-Files* fandom (aka X-Philes), who wanted to see Mulder and Scully admit what everyone else in the universe (*literally* the universe, what with the aliens and all) already knew. Supposedly the original word was *relationshipper* and the term we use today is a shortened version. Regardless, it's safe to say that humans have wanted to smoosh fictional people's faces together for a very long time. Perhaps one day we will all feel comfortable checking a census box that says "professional shipper," but many fangirls feel the stigma when it comes to being one. Annoyed nerd boys on an online message board introduced me to the term. Though I didn't know what the heck shippers were, I sure wasn't going to make the mistake of becoming one.

Now of course I chuckle to myself like an old man alone in a deli. I was a textbook shipper before I even knew what the term meant. So was it genetic or environmental? Could I have possibly heard the muffled squabbles of Sam and Diane in *Cheers* Season 3 while in utero? From the start, I paired everything and everyone. I shipped my teachers together and even historical figures (Lewis and Clark totally had a thing for each other). When a random street preacher warned of the rapture, I shuddered at the thought of Jesus coming back before my TV couples got together. Umm, *rude*.

If you grew up in the 1990s, it was impossible to escape without a ship. Of course there are the most famous ones, like Ross and Rachel. Buffy and Angel. Mulder and Scully. Doug and Carol. Obviously, that's a whole lot of straight white people. Fortunately, anything can happen on the Internet and because of that reality, the space is created for fans to ship whomever they damn well please. Two people from different TV shows? Done. Gender swaps? Done. Gay subtext? Triple done. Shipping helps people carve out their own identities and communicate them to the world, but it also doesn't limit them. Your own gender identity or sexual orientation doesn't always match what you choose to ship. I mean even the straightest person in the world could see that Rizzoli and Isles were super married to each other. Many slashfic writers are women. Love is love, and the fangirl knows it when she sees it on paper or screen. Here are some of the most common types of pairings you might find in the armada you've assembled.

S.S. RESPONSIBILITIES. Some of the best television ships blossom when two people work together but can't be together because of responsibilities. It's your classic co-worker pairing, where a twosome is too busy saving the universe, curing a patient, or catching a criminal to hear us shouting, *"Now kiss!"* When the feelings are repressed and not acknowledged, there's a heap of subtext you can use for fan fiction until the plot gets rolling and office supplies start flying off of desks.

NOSTALGIA CRUISE LINER. They've got history! You've got feels. Some of the most angsty but most satisfying ships are the ones where a couple had a fling in the past or missed their chance. And now, there's a chance that spark might reignite. This ship is great for writing flashback fic, but beware the dreaded love triangle that may plague the pairing on screen!

THE FORMER BROS BATTLESHIP. Totes bros! Or wait, maybe not? We all have those ships that start as bromance and evolve into something much, much more. This ship works particularly well for same-sex couples. Fangirls who serve on this vessel are quite hardy, because they have a lot of practice defending their ship to the naysayers.

SURPRISE SUBMARINE. You don't see it coming, and then, BOOM. Ships that hit you out of nowhere are sometimes the best ones, because there's no messy baggage they have to carry. Plus you can explore all those initial feels with some great fluffy fic writing sans angst. Squeeee!

OPPOSITES OUTRIGGER. I won't lie. This is my jam. Opposites are cliché, but nothing is better than an intellectual shouting match between two strong characters that results in make outs! Heroes and villains. Republicans and Democrats. Princesses and scoundrels. Whatever repels will attract when it comes to fic. Is it hot in here? Somebody grab the fire extinguisher.

We all have our preferences, but most fangirls can appreciate any kind of ship if it's well written in the canon or superbly imagined in the fandom (à la the crackship). However, like any aspect of the fangirl life, shipping carries its fair share of danger. Your intentions are honest, but your aim to maintain a healthy interest in a romantic pairing is worse than a drunken stormtrooper's. So when does shipping cease to be a safe mode of feeling your feels? When does it become a form of piracy that hijacks your ability to function well in your own relationships?

Ship Busters

Most of my fangirl friends don't expect their lives to be a fluff or angst or smut fest, but sometimes we all fall under the spell of absorbing too much Ephron or Austen-esque fiction. In this chapter, I'll parse out the differences between what makes a good fictional pairing and what makes a fantastic real-life ship. In order to root yourself in reality, first you have to take a look at some of the common shipping myths. So grab the nearest furry animal and hide your face in your hoodie, while we debunk the crap out of these plot devices.

THE *SINE QUA NON* MYTH. So let's start with the big guns, shall we? *Sine qua non* is a Latin legal term that roughly means, "without which it could not be." In short, the *Sine Qua Non* Myth teaches us that two people who are in love truly cannot exist without each other. Or as Carrie Bradshaw put it in *Sex and the City*, "Ridiculous, inconvenient, consuming, can't-live-without-each-other love." And we see this ideal modeled over and over again in fiction and television. Katniss and Peeta practically leap at the chance to die for the other. Think about the *Lost* finale, when various couples end up on the same pew together in Weird Church Heaven.

Yes, it's super romantic when a little old couple dies on the same day, but it's also a dangerous idealization. The concept of *sine qua non* pervades media, literature, music, and other arts. It is a gazillion-dollar industry, you readily empty your pockets, and Nicholas Sparks buys his ten millionth mini horse. But if people *really* gave up whenever they lost a person they thought was their true love, society would pretty much collapse.

Put the book really close to your face so I can tell you a secret about humans that you won't hear very often:

You, lady human, are really freaking resilient. Yes, you love intensely, but you also surmount the impossible with just as much strength, if not more.

In reality, the fear of losing your partner plays out quite unromantically. As a therapist, I have worked with a number of people who are guided by this anxiety of loss, which impacts their every thought and action. A person who is so intensely focused on someone else has little sense of identity. They freak out because a text isn't answered or they spend less time with their friends because they can't be apart from their partner. The irony is that this very fear is what causes most conflict in relationships, and constant togetherness is never as comforting. In fact it's quite suffocating.

Sine qua non is entertainment, and I don't see anything wrong with it in fiction, as long as you don't let the anxiety invested in two characters becoming canon guide your own decisions in relationships. Sure, very few of us would pay $14 to see a movie where the protagonist tells her love, "I'm happier with you in my life, but if I had to, I could live without you." It sounds harsh, but when we truly believe we can't live without another person, we spend our entire life operating out of the fear of potentially losing them. Your life must be guided by something stronger than fear or anxiety. So you can turn into Severus Snape and mope forever when your crush picks the wrong person or you can get up and move forward.

THE ANGSTY YELLING MYTH. Planted in front of the television, I grew up thinking that being in real love involved a lot of angsty shouting matches. So you could imagine my surprise when yelling at my elementary school crushes didn't quite pan out. Most of us are susceptible to picking smaller fights or arguments with our romantic partner or our crush. We confuse the emotional volatility in an argument with the excitement that attraction or perhaps even love promotes between two people, and we settle for the lesser version.

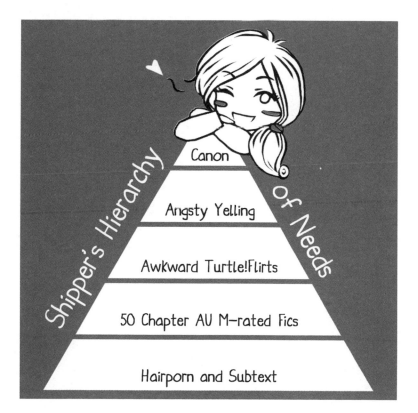

But in fiction, conflict makes for sexy plot. If you don't think a good argument is fictional foreplay, then you've never seen *The Empire Strikes Back*, or a single Katharine Hepburn movie. Debunking this myth is somewhat painful for me, because I am all about idiots who yell at each other. Who doesn't love a good *Much Ado*–style bout of back and forth before two people start going at it?

In real life, people who can't stand the sight of each other usually don't shout because they are secretly in love. They usually scream at each other because they become extremely reactive to the smallest of things. They become irrational, overwhelmed with feelings of persecution or fear. There's nothing sexy about losing your ability to think for yourself in a relationship because you're so overcome with rage. So let's just leave this one in our angsty fanfics, okay?

THE SUBTEXT MYTH. As the great George Costanza once said, "It's not a lie if you believe it." Oh subtext. What would we do without you? Armadas of ships have been launched from a single glance or a hand brush between characters. For those unfamiliar with the concept of subtext, here is my personal set of subtext rules for TV characters.

- If they make eye contact, they are in love
- If they refuse to make eye contact, they are in love
- If they are alone in a room together, they are in love

- If they stand within three feet of each other, they are in love

- If they yell at each other, they are in love

- If they say sassy things to each other, they are in love

- If they are wearing matching colors, they are in love

- If they openly hate each other, they are in love

As you can see, the field is ripe for subtext reading. Subtext is the crackshipper's best friend in particular. Why is crackshipping so popular, particularly when there's so little physical evidence available? Fangirls love the thrill of the idea that any pairing can become plausible with good fan fiction and some people's God-given manip-making talents. They're experts at convincing just about anyone that the tiniest spark is a supernova.

So what's the problem with subtext? Doesn't it exist in real life? I'd be out of a job if it didn't. But it is trickier to successfully identify in real life. Sometimes people have a tendency to translate a potential partner's lack of interest into subtext. Fiction is our Rumpelstiltskin, convincing us that we can spin subtext out of a giant pile of nothing. You might find yourself daydreaming about a crush pining over you, or interpreting a kind gesture a certain way, and the lines between this fiction and reality increasingly blur.

As exciting as a crush can be, your own ship story should be about what is there and what is spoken, not what you daydream. Using subtext as evidence in relationships will result only in a lot of hurt and regret. If someone likes you, for the love of ships please make sure he or she demonstrates that to you, because showing up at work wearing the same color shirt is not sufficient. Don't be *The Mortal Instruments's* Simon mooning over Clary when she's clearly mooning after Jace.

THE TROPE MYTH. Every fangirl knows that the best stories are the ones with the fewest tropes, where characters challenge our assumptions about how they react or the roles they will play as their stories develop. Real life is no different; relationships struggle when we limit ourselves to stereotypical patterns. Take for example the classic heterosexual sitcom marriage. The wife takes on too many responsibilities, ending up resenting herself and her partner. Life is not an episode of *Everybody Loves Raymond*, so it's not funny when you feel like the scale is off balance in your love life.

Another appealing relationship trope is what I call the Sorkin neurotic and her suitor. Fangirls are particularly susceptible to gravitating toward the neurotic. We're more self-conscious, we struggle to delay gratification, and it often takes very small amounts of stress to send our heads spinning. We can also become confused when funny, endearing fictional folks embody these traits. TV writers love to write neurotic women, but in real life, nobody wants to deal with a dysfunctional personality. "Oh look, I can't regulate my emotions. Isn't that adorable?" No.

No it is not. As much as you might romanticize all your quirks, chances are your obsessions, anxieties, and jealousies are not cute added features like the flower vase in a Volkswagen Beetle. They are maladaptive behaviors that will hurt you and any relationship you enter.

Perhaps the most appealing is the trope of the Unicorn lovers. Many of us millennials were raised to believe in our unicorn nature. And many young women start their sentences with "I'm not like one of those girls who does X, Y, Z." But in the real world, no one's going to give you an award or sweep you off your feet simply because you wear T-shirts when she wears short skirts. Because you've read Proust when your friends are reading John Green. There are a thousand other Rory Gilmores out there. So for the love of BAMFs, stop telling people you're cooler because you liked Fleetwood Mac before everyone else. Chances are you weren't even alive in 1977. If we know anything about being fangirls, it's that we are never the *only* person who thinks that one show or that one book is cool. That is the whole point. Yes, your significant other should make you feel like a unicorn. But don't be surprised if he or she won't hang around if you're constantly dismissing others as less-than.

When I think about all the women who are on my BAMF list, most of them have healthy relationships because they don't fall into these tropes. Yes there are fireworks and squee-worthy moments, but the ship doesn't have to put a woman in boxes like these to achieve them. The best fictional relationships on television, the Ben Wyatts and the Leslie Knopes, happen when people can be vulnerable without sacrificing their uniqueness. When people are committed to working on themselves as much as their partner is committed to loving them.

Imaginary Make Outs

Fangirls can participate in a lot of self-deprecating humor about being forever single with their cats (and there is absolutely nothing wrong with that) or forever being in a relationship with a fictional character. You may say that no real person could truly relate to your fangirl nature. A young woman once wrote to me asking how to stop imagining making out with famous YouTubers and band members. "I snog my hand pretending it's them," she wrote. "Whenever I'm out places I picture myself walking with them. I'm scared that the next time a boy likes me, I'll go too far since I keep looking for unrealistic love. How do I stop doing this do myself?"

I assured this reader that making out with your hand is developmentally on point for any teenager, young adult, or congressman. And that writing yourself into fic or headcanon isn't unhealthy either. (I too have starred in any number of Emmy-winning television shows when I'm trying to fall asleep at night.) My advice was that instead of focusing on how famous dude crushes are unrealistic, she needed to think about how her kissy dreams can provide her some valuable information about herself. What was different about the band member's girlfriend and her current hand-snogging self? Were there any character traits she would like to embody or improve?

When I think of the daydream, in love version of myself, a couple of differences stand out. Daydream Me is braver, kinder to others, and more vulnerable in her relationships. She doesn't lurch around muttering sarcastic comments, and she's not so hard on herself. This is a signal to me that these are the character traits I value above all others whether single or in a relationship. That there are more appealing aspects of a ship than just yelling, and that you can be a better romantic partner because of them. Your personal life doesn't have to be as messy as Olivia Pope's to be exciting.

So if you're a single fangirl looking for the other half of your ship, I'd recommend this: Rather than worrying about going cold turkey on the imaginary feels, see how your dreams can generate a map for your own character development. Your plot arc may not have sexy times for a good while, but who cares when you're so awesome! You can make out with life while you're waiting for the right person to come along. When you're being brave and striving to be the best draft of yourself, people will notice. Who knows? They might even start to imagine themselves kissing you.

Achieving OTP Status

Let's say that you've found someone who wants to make out with you for the long haul. Being in an OTP-worthy relationship means being loved and accepted for your fangirl nature, but you must also challenge yourself to love and respect your partner for his or her different interests. Here are some common mistakes you might make in a twosome, and how to avoid them.

ARDENT EVANGELIZING. If you really love a TV show or a book, then woot. Love it. But don't expect your dude or lady to want to watch everything you watch or to watch it with the same level of enthusiasm. Internet folks are there to welcome you with open arms so you can get your Delena creys on. There's a difference between recommending a show and embarking on an evangelistic mission to convert your partner, and avoiding the latter is likely to save you a lot of anxiety.

DON'T BE HALF-PRESENT. Don't be that couple who's looking at their smartphones through the entirety of dinner. Prioritize real people over fictional ones. You'll survive if you miss an episode or people's immediate reactions to an *Orphan Black* spoiler. You don't have to have a TV in the bedroom. When you're half-watching a show, you miss the great parts, right? The same applies to life and love. When you're half-present in your relationship, you miss some really great moments.

RESPECT DIFFERENCES. Don't tease your partner for not knowing what a fangirl word is or who an actor is. If he or she relates to a different character, then respect that relationship. If your partner prefers not to be spoiled and you love to know what's going to happen three episodes from now, then keep your mouth shut. My boyfriend didn't know about the Red Wedding, and I didn't peep a word. So summon that willpower.

EMOTIONAL RESPONSIBILITY. It is not your partner's job to calm you down if you get all worked up about a plot twist or an Internet hater. Don't project your anger and take it out on the person you love. You don't have to hide who you are, and you can share your feelings, but you do need to take responsibility for yourself like the good BAMF that you are.

If you're thanking me for ruining romance for you, you're very much welcome. The great things about love become greater when you create the space to be yourself rather than constantly flail about when conflicts occur. So now that you have a pretty solid idea of what behaviors you should avoid, you might be wondering what real relationships actually look like when they become a one true pairing. In my work, I like to imagine that there are three key ingredients: Openness, Trust, and Parity. Yes, that's right, I made a corny acronym. You can be an A+ shipper while maintaining your own healthy relationships. All you have to do is follow the OTP Model.

OPENNESS. Being open does not mean you share every thought you have about Sansa Stark's character development with your partner. It's more about being able to communicate what you value in a thoughtful way. Partners who are open don't always agree, but they do choose to share rather than distance themselves from the problem. The tricky part is figuring out when you should share and solve a problem together and when you need to handle your own feels. The key is that if your instinct is to distance yourself or hide the facts from your partner, then it's probably something you need to be open about. Like when you were supposed to wait for your partner to watch the latest episode of *Veep* but you didn't because you are so, very, very weak. Whoops.

TRUST. When you operate out of fear of losing another person, it is very difficult to trust him or her. But when you take responsibility for yourself and remember what a resilient little creature you are, you're less likely to be afraid. You can trust your significant other to not cheat, lie, or make dumb decisions. If your partner does violate your trust, you are mentally prepared to decide how to react. Trusting isn't about finding the perfect person. It's about knowing what you can and can't control. You can't control your partner's actions any more than you can keep J. K. Rowling from tweeting unnecessary character information. So give your partner the space for his or her own story. You're not going to share every scene with him or her, but you can believe that what's good for your partner's story is good for your relationship.

PARITY. Having an equal relationship is less about making sure the chores and the check are divided in half and more about not taking over for the other person. Lack of parity can sneak up on you, with a bunch of small things that add up. If you're making sure your partner wakes up on time, remembers appointments, finishes homework, and so on, then you don't have parity. The seesaw is tilted, and you're carrying more of the load. Sure, a good relationship is about helping each other, but sometimes we help too much. Two grownups should be able to adult as a couple and as individuals.

If you have OTP in your relationship, you'll feel more confident, your romantic partner will feel less pressure, and you'll enjoy spending time together rather than wasting it fighting another battle. Yes we're suckers for the six-season unrequited love arc, but if you look closely, you'll see that many of the fictional characters you ship exhibit many of these characteristics of a functional real-life relationship. Lasting relationships happen when two people learn from one another and cheer for each other but also give each other the freedom and space to be their authentic selves. They can be together, but they can also be apart, and who wouldn't ship that? To jump-start your thinking about healthy relationships, here are three quick exercises you can do today.

TROPE VACCINATION. Sometimes you can fall into the same old stereotypes that make for bad television and bad relationships. You know yourself well enough to guess which stereotypes you're most susceptible to in a relationship. So why wait until symptoms manifest to start to do something about it? If you're in danger of becoming a passive-aggressive sitcom wife, then speak openly and listen to your partner. If you see yourself evolving into a neurotic Sorkin-esque female, then text a friend a code word to help talk you down when you're being irrational. Tropes can feel comfortable, but they tempt us to stop working on the parts of ourselves that need polishing.

OTP CHERRY-PICK. Set a timer for sixty seconds and write down all the pairings you ship. Pick two pairings, and write down the characteristics of the relationship. Separate the mythic characteristics (factors that wouldn't work in the real world) from the real characteristics. Of the real, admirable characteristics, choose several that you can think about and apply to your own relationships.

BAMF PLAYLIST. As always, you can borrow courage from fiction. Your favorite ladies make plenty of bold moves when they're dating, enjoying being single, or working out problems in relationships. Make a top ten list of the most badass moves your girl crushes have made when it comes to love, and pick a few to try out for yourself. Maybe you'll ask out a stranger or enjoy a solo date with yourself!

CHAPTER 7
HATERS AND HELPERS

> Fangirls are all a-holes a little bit.
>
> —AME, TWENTY-FOUR

> Why are you the way that you are? Honestly, every time I try to do something fun or exciting, you make it not that way. I hate so much about the things that you choose to be.
>
> —MICHAEL SCOTT, *THE OFFICE*

It's the hard-knock life for the fangirl, or at least it can seem that way. Once a day we just want to throw the towel in because it's easier than putting up a fight with the haters. Haters look like the guy in your second-period class who mocks the Bellamy/Clarke background on your laptop. Or your boss who doesn't get why you write *Doctor Who* fic on your lunch break. This fear of the meanies encourages us to hide our identity as fangirls. We're deemed pathetic or not capable of operating in reality, and sometimes we begin to consider whether that's the truth. Fangirls sometimes struggle to distinguish between who will embrace them, who is there to pick a fight, and who can really help them on their journey. So naturally, you might feel the need to hide from everyone. I want to make sure you leave this chapter knowing when to poke your head out of your shell and dance around and when you should scoot on down the road. We'll explore how to be your authentic self with loved ones, when to ignore the haters, and how to find the helpers who can give you real feedback as you grow.

A teenager emailed me recently with a great question. "My friends and I are all fangirls, and we were wondering if you could help us with how to tell our parents and family. How do we deal with those weird people that just don't understand us?" Oh, those weird people. They just don't get it, do they? I have to admit that I too was guilty of letting the fangirl stigma prevent me from being more open about my passions with those closest to me. What is ironic, however, is the realization that I have never really gotten many raised eyebrows when I have been open about my interests. Family and friends think my dedication to middle-aged women and their hair is quirky, funny, and maybe a little confusing. But they would probably use those words to describe my personality anyway. The truth is that the majority of people will love you and accept you when you're living the best fangirl life that you can live. They'll still come to you for advice even though they know you have three hundred pictures of Lorde on your iPhone.

So how do you live openly as a fangirl? The only way to test the waters and your bravery is to just shout your fan fever from the rooftops. Okay, maybe at a lower volume and a lower elevation. Casual, everyday conversation is the best way to share your passions with the world. Don't tell me the opportunity never presents itself, because it always does. A simple, "How are you doing?" can be your entry point to trot in like the little unicorn that you are. Here are a few other examples of how you can infuse fangirling into regular humanspeak.

- **PERSON AT A DINNER PARTY:** What do you do?

- **ME:** I cry about hair and gay subtext. What do you do?

. . . .

- **NON-FANGIRL FRIEND:** How's life going?

- **ME:** AMAZE. My OTP had sex in a car this week! *Pterodactyl screech*

• •

- **ELDERLY GRANDPARENT WITHOUT WI-FI:** What would you like to do today?

- **ME:** Can you drive me to the McDonald's parking lot so I can update my SwanQueen fanfic? My readers are getting impatient.

• •

But let's be serious. There are millions of opportunities to introduce your fangirlness into everyday conversation. What about the dreaded circle of sharing in a new class? Tell them you have a Tumblr dedicated to Alex Kingston's hair. Your dad asks you why you're texting so furiously? Explain that you're engaged in a lively debate about sorting your high school teachers into Hogwarts houses. In short, just *say* what you're doing. (Unless you're researching weird sex things for fic, then please dear god, don't say what you're doing.) I can guarantee you that ninety-nine times out of a hundred it will sound more fun than whatever your inquisitor is doing. She will be curious, jealous, or confused enough that she'll back away slowly and leave you in peace.

I keep my fangirling
strictly to the internet

9%

Everyone knows
I'm a fangirl
33%

52%
A few people
in real life know
but I don't tell
them everything

6%
No one
knows

How out are you about your fangirling?

A funny thing will happen when you start living in a more authentic way. Other people around you feel more comfortable doing the same. Yes, there are real live meanies out there who might tease or criticize you for livin' life like a true fangirl. But I would argue that most of the time, those critical voices are Carl in disguise. He's dressing up like your friends and your colleagues and romping around your mind with that giant megaphone. "Don't be different!" he shouts. "Fit in with the group!"

Remember, Carl's arguments would never hold up in fangirl court. Like Jon Snow, he knows nothing.

Communicating fangirlhood to friends and family also is about quality, not quantity. If you talk about your lady loves nonstop on all social media and in every conversation, then you're going to annoy the crap out of everyone. Different fangirls have different limits. I have a constant group text with three friends where we dump our fangirl emotions. I call them "the committee." Have emotions? Discuss them with the committee. That way you know you won't overwhelm other friends or your significant other with feels upon feels upon feels. So yes, some degree of compartmentalizing is helpful. Conversely, your role is also not to be a hater toward people who don't get *quite* as excited as you do. Respect the friends who waited to watch *Downton Abbey* when it premiered in the United States, when you gave ITV a fake Welsh postal code five months earlier (hypothetical example; I would *never* do that, ITV).

The Troll Whisperer

So friends and family are one challenge. But the Internet is a completely different landscape. For the novice, Fangirl World might appear to be this happy little island where we all play nice in the sand, fawning over characters and ships and hair without tripping over each other's egos. But you are not a novice, are you? You know that eventually the clouds roll in, and that there are just as many haters lurking inside every corner of fandom as there are skeptics who mock your way of life. The resident fandom villain stalks the Internet, waiting to pounce and spew her pettiness all over you like a demon being exorcised. Those of you living on the periphery of fandom land may think I'm exaggerating, but the rest of you have encountered this creature in one form or another. She is a fangirl, but she is also a Grade A troll.

Fandom haters are the girls who go all Somali pirate on the ships they don't like or the girls who make fun of you when you try to mimic your girl crush's hairstyle. They act like they own a show or a character, insist they know more than you do, and write dissertation-long posts to try to prove it. Resident fandom dictators, they try to engage new fans by spewing hate about other fangirls, and occasionally they find a few other haters and gang up to wreak havoc in a fandom. Their immaturity leaves a taste in your mouth so foul that you consider giving up being a fan all together. We've all been at that fork in the road at one time or another where we question whether our interests are worth the cost of these people.

So why don't we develop an immunity over time? Why do some fangirls annoy the crap out of us so, so much? Because we think irrationally about how the Internet should function and how we must act as fangirls. Albert Ellis, one of the fathers of cognitive-behavioral therapy, said there are three core beliefs that can cause problems for humans. These beliefs are just as true for fangirls roaming through the wilds of the Internet.

IRRATIONAL BELIEF 1: YOU MUST BE LOVED BY EVERYONE IN YOUR COMMUNITY. Raise your

hand if you've been personally victimized by someone on the Internet. If you operate under the assumption that every person in a fandom will welcome you with open arms, then you are in for a rude awakening. People will dislike you for good reasons and for not so good reasons, but you get wound up regardless. You rush to your circle of fandom friends to lick your wounds and speak ill of that horrible stan who shamed you.

IRRATIONAL BELIEF 2: YOU MUST EXCEL AT EVERYTHING. When you put pressure on yourself to be

the first person to post a red carpet pic, the best fic writer, the fastest gif maker, and the funniest Tweeter, you're bound to encounter someone who's just a teensy bit more skilled than you are. This sets you up for Internet brawling and feelings of intense jealousy. The reality is that you may be missing out on a friendship that could actually be quite wonderful.

IRRATIONAL BELIEF 3: CERTAIN PEOPLE ARE BAD AND MUST BE PUNISHED. We are quick to label

people we've never met in fandom. But everyone's a troll on a bad day. It might seem like haters want their words to burrow into your brain, but take a step back and try to be objective about the situation. Above all, be empathetic. You probably don't know their life situation, or the obstacles they've faced. Though unhealthy, their actions may be a coping mechanism for whatever crap circumstances they face every day. You can be kind without condoning the behavior. But how?

In real life, what do we tend to do with people who make us too anxious or ragey because of the differences in our values and opinions? We cut them out, right? Social psychologists will tell you that "Like likes like," so we tend to gather around others who are similar to us. What I want to recommend to you is kind of controversial, but the most challenging advice usually is. I want you to try an experiment. Whenever you encounter someone on the Internet who has a different opinion than you do, I don't want you to hit the unfollow button or block them.

The problem with cutting people off is that it does not erase our rage. It's only a temporary solution. Therapists recommend that people maintain relationships with difficult family members or colleagues, even when it's hard. If this sounds bonkers to you, think about how a religious cult might operate. What's one of the first things they ask people to do? Cut off from family members and friends who don't agree with them. If, as a fangirl, you can teach yourself to communicate with people who disagree with you, you might find yourself able to do it calmly and thoughtfully. You'll find that you'll be able to take a position yourself without feeling the need to force another person into your camp. You'll be able to crush any topic without needing your rage.

Over time, this ability to communicate without raging can become a veritable BAMF skill. Families, societies, governments, and even fandoms work best when leaders choose to maintain contact with those who disagree with them—even those people who aren't that polite about it. I'm not suggesting you follow everyone on Tumblr who shipped Ted and Robin or call a relative to talk about politics right this second. What I do recommend is that you pay attention to your clicky finger. What does the clicky finger tell you about your emotions? Is it quick to knock people out of your social circles, or are you willing to share your thoughts without hatred and see what might happen? It's hard work, but it does make a difference. With enough time and practice, you'll find that your fangirl rage will cool and evolve into mild annoyance, and eventually into intriguing conversation. And your attitude might inspire the people you're communicating with to do the same.

Policing the Internet

So let's say you see hate on the Internet, but it's not directed at you. What is your responsibility as a fangirl? Do you call the haters out or do you ignore them? Maybe you have strong political beliefs, passions about human rights, or specialized knowledge in a particular field. Maybe you're just someone with common sense. If you use the Internet, it is inevitable that you will encounter entire villages of jerks. Fangirls are especially vulnerable, because we can get riled up for a number of reasons. Here are just a few.

FANGIRL RAGE TRIGGERS

- Questionable character interpretations

- Ships or fic that promote unhealthy relationships

- Homophobia, racism, sexism, ageism, all the -phobias and -isms

- Arrogance about knowing a show or book better than everyone else

- Stalking behavior toward celebrities

- Saying hateful things and tagging them for others to see

So let's say you see someone complaining about a ship being "too old," or maybe they're using abusive plot in their fan fiction. Is it your job to correct everyone's thinking on the Internet, or even in a fandom?

Nope. No, it's not. I'm going to say this once, and then I won't say it again. It is not your job to police the Internet. I bet you want to police me right now for saying that, but let me explain! I'm a licensed mental health counselor. And you can imagine how many times I see erroneous information about mental health on Tumblr. So do I send a five-paragraph essay to every person who posts something wrong about depression? I want to, but I don't. Because—say it with me—*It's not my job to police the Internet.* Oops, sorry, I had to say it again. Just so you got it. Got it?

"But Kathleeeen. There are people who are wrong in their wrongness out there, and if I don't correct them, how will they know they are so very, very wrong?" Well let's take a step back and check your motivation. Internet police aren't doing it to help someone be a better person. They're doing it to be seen calling people out and to feel right in their rightness. Which, I'd argue, is also a type of bullying. If we've already positioned ourselves against another person, then we're just contributing to that polarization that exists on the Internet and beyond.

"But Kathleen. I.REALLY.HAVE.TO.TELL.THEM." Okay fine. Then send it in a private message. Tell them you value X and why. Don't tell them why they're wrong or make it a personal attack. Tell them why you've experienced the subject differently. Why you personally preferred the Tenth Doctor to the Eleventh Doctor. Speak about you, because you can't speak for them. If you limit yourself to reaching out to folks only privately, then ninety-nine times out of a hundred you've lost the desire to call them out. Because in the end, it was about only you in the first place, wasn't it?

In case you need science to believe me, a few years ago the University of Michigan did a study to see whether people changed their minds when they were presented with contradictory facts. Spoiler alert—they didn't. In fact, we are more likely to cling to our false beliefs like a dubious season finale spoiler than consider the contrary. This phenomenon is known as *back-fire*, and it explains why certain groups believe that people rode dinosaurs around three thousand years ago. Or that Beth didn't die on *The Walking Dead*. Sure, kids. Sure.

You cannot change the world with facts alone. You cannot change the world by winning an argument with every racist relative you have on Facebook. People's hearts and minds are changed when they hear or experience a narrative that challenges their worldview. That process starts with you listening to other people's stories and allowing your own beliefs to be challenged and edited. If we don't examine our own biases, then how do we even know that we're not the villains in our own story or someone else's?

How do you transform Internet rage into something positive? Let me issue you a challenge. Every time you feel tempted to engage with someone in a volatile way on the Internet, I want you to donate a dollar to a local charity. Walk outside and pick up a piece of litter in your neighborhood. Call people you haven't spoken to in a while and tell them you love them. Help a kid with her fractions. Do anything as long as it puts something positive into the world. Don't fight negativity with more negativity. Whether you're religious or not, having faith means believing that kindness is stronger than hate.

Maybe you are stomping your foot down and clamping your mouth shut, because you just can't bring yourself to be kind to that Internet meanie. Then go and be kind to someone else, and eventually that muscle will grow strong enough. If you're living a life that speaks more truth than an Internet comment, then people might surprise you and loosen their grip a little on their beliefs. Or maybe they won't. But it was never your job to pry their hands apart. "Lighthouses don't go running all over an island looking for boats to save," writes Anne Lamott. "They just stand there shining."

Taking Feedback

So, what if someone calls *you* out for something? What about that, huh? Everyone's talking these days about how younger generations don't know how to take feedback. There is *some* truth to the argument. I've taught graduate students who expect A's for simply showing up and keeping their faces glued to their phones the entire time. Heck, I *was* a graduate student who expected that. Like any good ship, feedback and I have a complicated history, but we're learning to live together. For a long time, I was a baby writer who expected every editor to look at my first draft and go, "Oh my god! This is perfect. Thank you for existing!" Basically the reaction you have when you watch Viola Davis in anything. Instead I might get something like, "Good start," and I'd open the Word document to find it bloodied with Track Changes as the "Rains of Castamere" played softly in the background.

Over time, I realized that the people who challenged me were not creeping Walder Freys. I became a better counselor when I urged my clients to speak up when they weren't happy with our work together. If you want to ignore or refuse feedback, you'll probably never be more than *kinda sorta* good at anything you do. You can hide from criticism or you can open the floodgates and take it like a woman. Over time, you'll become even better than you thought you could be.

Now that doesn't mean that authentic feedback won't hurt. We ask people we respect for their honest opinion, and then get angry with them when that's exactly what they give us. How dare they not say your Caskett fic is the greatest literary work since *Heat Wave*! How dare they think your fave is problematic! So, what shall you do to thicken your skin? Lucky for you, incorporating feedback is yet another skill that can be assembled with help from the fangirl tool belt. You probably already know a buttload of fictional people who have improved with feedback from someone invested in their improvement. Here are just a few.

CHARACTER	FEEDBACK COACH
Katniss Everdeen	Haymitch Abernathy
Buffy Summers	Rupert Giles
Beatrix Kiddo	Pai Mei
Harry Potter	Albus Dumbledore
Liz Lemon	Jack Donaghy
Luke Skywalker	Yoda

So two things we notice here. One is that all the mentors are male. What is up with that? We're seeing a rise of the female mentors in some TV shows, but for the most part, dudes give fictional feedback. Leslie Knope was a great start, but we've got to figure out a way to change this dynamic. Change it, fangirls! Demand lady mentors.

The second thing you'll notice is that none of these coaches are particularly warm and fuzzy people. Sure Dumbledore has got the grandpa thing going on, but he can be quite a BAMF himself. If you want to improve yourself and work toward a goal, you have to have a Yoda in your life who is willing to ask you to try it again or even maybe cut your ego down a notch or two. I appreciate people who take what I give them and run with it, but the ones who say, "You can do better. Let's try this again," are the ones that make the real difference.

Then there are the people who will actively criticize you when they have zero investment in your future. How do you tell if someone is giving you useful criticism or is just being a meanie? A meanie critiques you as a person rather than the behavior or idea itself. She'll disguise insults as compliments, and she doesn't care when you send a thoughtful response to the critique. Here are just a few meanie remarks I've gotten over the years.

- This is actually less than good advice

- This writer owes us all an apology

- Perhaps you aren't worth as much as you think you are

- Sometimes Kathleen gets too excited and forgets there are other students in the class

Okay, that last one was from my first-grade report card, but you get the idea. Again, meanies sound a lot like our old pal Carl. They're not fact-oriented creatures. They are the haters who feel threatened because you've chosen to live outside the norm, because they can't take advantage of you, or just because they have no other hobbies. When you start making bold moves, it will drive some people bananas. They'll tell you you've made a huge mistake. They'll send you emails with frowny face emoticons. You just go ahead, print that email, and hang it up on your wall to remind you that not everyone will agree with the way you live your life. But those people aren't enough reason for you to stop moving forward. There will always be Malfoys and President Snows in this world, and if you're not careful, you'll let them dictate how your story will be told.

So keep swimming, and keep disappointing people. Listen to your mentors and the people who root for you, and remember that they're the ones with your best interests at heart, even when they challenge you. The desire to fit in is super strong, but if you're constantly making readjustments to fit in with the group, you'll lose track of your own plot development. Taking a BAMF stance means saying, "Hey, here's what I believe. Here's what I like. This is me. And if you disagree, let's talk about it like civilized folks." Here are a few exercises to help you with just that.

HATER MIRROR. Think of all the haters you have encountered in your fandom adventures, both fangirls and outsiders. Write down all the negative qualities that you don't like about them. Here comes the gross part! Circle all of those qualities that you sometimes exhibit yourself, both inside and outside of fandom life. Pick one of those character traits and examine how you could start acting differently in your relationships. Consider what characteristics in your favorite BAMF could replace this not so attractive part of yourself. How would your life be different?

ACTIVATE UNICORN FEATURES. Make a list of five important people in your life who don't know much about your fangirl activities. Beside each person's name, describe how you think she might react if you shared more about your feels. Pick three of these people and plan how you can introduce your fangirlness into your next conversation with them. Remember that you can be professional and still have a little squee from time to time. So enjoy being a unicorn!

FIND YOUR YODA. The best way to learn to take your feedback vitamins is to ask for them. Find a friend or colleague you respect and ask her for her feedback about your work. Practice not arguing with her point of view and limit yourself to the words *thank you*. Take a close look at the criticism and see what you can gain from it. If it helps, imagine your favorite literary mentor voicing these opinions. Remember, the goal isn't to be right or perfect, but to be able to hear other points of view and see them as a challenge for growth.

CHAPTER 8
DEATH AND STUFF

> When I fall asleep in Mrs. Detrolio's class tomorrow, someone tell her that it's because I stayed up all night crying about people dying on *Lost*.
>
> **—BRITTANY, NINETEEN**

> Embrace the probability of your imminent death, and know in your heart that there's nothing I can do to save you.
>
> **—HAYMITCH ABERNATHY, *THE HUNGER GAMES***

Life changes in an instant. You blink and everything that is safe and familiar just slips through your fingers. One minute I was curled up on the couch in my sophomore dorm room, celebrating the end of finals by blasting through another DVD of *Friends* Season 7. Seconds later I found myself digging through my closet; black sweaters, black skirts, black heels floated into my suitcase. My phone buzzed again, and I ducked my head underneath the bunk bed to sit down.

"Mom didn't make it. You need to get a flight home."

My roommates and I rode in silence to the airport, the cab surfing through the January slush of Boston. One of them tucked a Ziploc bag of Kleenex into my backpack as my brain assessed whether my bag would make it through security. "Is an eyelash curler considered a weapon?" I joked. A female security guard patted me down after I triggered the alarm. Didn't she know that my mother had just died? I no longer had to wonder when I would begin to feel like an adult. The line in the sand separating my childhood from the rest of my life had been drawn.

I know what you're thinking. You bought this book to read about hairporn and have fuzzy girl power emotions. Not to be reminded that everything and everyone you love will end someday or to contemplate the inevitable heat death of the universe. Or the reality that *Supernatural* will finally be put out of its misery sometime around Season 78. But the truth is, a story by its very nature comes to an end. You wouldn't pick up a book if the pages never stopped multiplying, and living life is no different. You will encounter people both real and fictional whose stories will end long before yours, so grief is a natural and unavoidable part of your existence. Grief changes you like an ominous *Alice's Adventures in Wonderland* beverage—things that once seemed important often feel rather trivial. "If I can get through this," you say, "then nothing will be that difficult." But after a decade, I've found that there is no "through." You're always in it, but so is everyone else at one point or another.

Grief is a topic that isn't discussed much in fangirl world. When we talk about character death, it's almost always a joke: How funny our meltdown can be when we lose *yet another* person to the fictional graveyard. How we must hate ourselves because we keep signing up for more pain. When other people think of fandom, they point to shipping, or actor worship, but fangirls are also experts at loss. To quote *The X-Files*, our conscience is the dead speaking to us. So what does that one life-ruining character death speak to you and your life? Let's figure that out. In this chapter we'll take a look at how character death can impact and inform our lives, and you'll learn how to be a resilient fangirl. Then we'll talk about what happens the day your favorite show ends, and how to move forward. Finally, we will prepare for the spinoffs of real life and plan how to handle transitions like a pro. There is value in the pain, because grief can prompt a whole new way of thinking and living. You just have to sit up and pay attention to it.

Here Lies Every Character
I Ever Loved

Did you know that Shonda Rhimes is the leading cause of character death? I'm kidding! We all know it's good old George R. R. Martin. Nobody is safe, especially anyone adopted into Dean Winchester's family circle. Writers rub out characters due to plot points or impatient actors, and they seldom stop to consider the wake of ever-loving emotions they leave in their path of destruction. Because we seem to wring some semblance of meaning from the experience or because we like self-flagellation, the fangirl keeps coming back for more. Some of us are unlucky in love because we always choose favorite characters who die. The "imagine your OTP" meme is laughable to us, because we're still working on "imagine your OTP is alive."

When people ask me if a fictional death can be just as bad as a real one, I'm quick to point out that grief isn't a competition. The fact that losing a family member typically has more of an impact doesn't cancel out other forms of grief. Unfortunately, however, society doesn't always acknowledge some losses as being significant, such as the death of a pet or a miscarriage. In the therapy world, this phenomenon is known as disenfranchised grief, and certainly the fictional character death falls under this category. Not being able to talk openly about the loss and not having a strong social network can both complicate grief, leading the fangirl to feel more angry and confused when her emotions are dismissed as superficial or dramatic.

Thanks to the Internet, fangirls have created a space to grieve the fictional greats. Different cultures have different traditions for mourning their dead, and fandom is no exception. Sure, you'll flail about in the ball pit of denial for a bit, but eventually you begin the process of mourning. Here are some common behaviors exhibited by the fangirl when she grieves a dead fictional person.

- Frequent posting of death scene gifs

- Surfing Etsy to purchase jewelry symbolic of dead character

- Hibernating to read lengthy AU fanfics late into the night

- Missing work or school the day after the death

- Creating "sad panda" fanmixes that are played repeatedly

- Abstaining from proper hygiene practices and/or healthy eating

There is nothing wrong with these behaviors in the short term. But when you perform them in isolation, rather than seeing the deeper gift behind loss, you miss the point entirely. I've had a lot of characters die on me over the years, but none of them were quite like Laura Roslin in *Battlestar Galactica* (don't you dare complain about spoilers, you hermit, the show's been over for years). I wailed. I assumed the fetal position. My roommate probably thought I sounded like a dying raccoon through the wall. So the next day I got up and did the only natural thing: I surrounded myself with online friends who were also knee deep in heartbreak. The experience was sort of like an instant support group that never adjourned. We were all part of a family who had lost a treasured fictional member.

Many of our favorite TV shows wrestle with questions of existence and purpose, and in order do to that, people have to check out from time to time. Or in the case of *Game of Thrones*, every freaking episode. Death plots explore how we make meaning of human stories that will inevitably come to an end. In *BSG*, what the Cylons want more desperately than anything else is to be like humans but also maintain their immortal status. What they initially fail to realize is that our mortality is what makes us human, and that stories are stories because they end. Rather than fear relationships because they end in separation, this reality should inspire us to pursue them. Sure, sometimes actors get bored and end up cutting a character's life short because they want to leave the show, and the deaths don't have that much meaning in the grand scheme of the story. But in witnessing the death, often you will find that you can carry away something more than tears alone. Here are just a few of my takeaways from character deaths that affected me. You could write an essay for each one, but I'll try to sum it up in a few words.

CHARACTER DEATH	MY TAKEAWAY
Laura Roslin, *BSG*	Life can have meaning in the face of death
Andrea, *The Walking Dead*	Believe in the goodness of everyone
Fred Weasley, *Harry Potter*	Make time to be completely ridiculous
Rue, *The Hunger Games*	Help those who can't speak for themselves
Ned Stark, *Game of Thrones*	Pay attention to what your parents do right
Juliet Burke, *Lost*	TV writers are horrible people

So that's a nice list of fictional pain, but what does this have to do with *actual* death? When a character dies the actor is still around or we can just pick up the book again or write fic. When we die . . . well, people have a lot of different opinions about that. So let's take a second and think about death. About there being an end date on your Wikipedia page. A sobering thought. Teenagers often feel invincible, eager to grow up as time drags on as slowly as a midseason hiatus. Eventually, however, you might begin to consider that maybe your life isn't turning out how you imagined. The fangirl tends to react to this dissonance in a predictable manner. She burrows her head deeper into fictional worlds, making her characters say the words and perform the actions she wishes could be her own.

When you make the decision to bury yourself in fiction, there is little energy left over to effect real change. Over time, the difference between your actual self and your ideal self will grow wider and wider. Yes, characters are a brilliant starting point for generating thoughts and revving up your imagination, but at some point you have to consider the plot of your own narrative. Life is much messier and more mundane than fiction at times, but it is also more satisfying when the seemingly impossible is achieved. It is both horrible and wonderful to be real, isn't it?

Death isn't a reason to just be sad. It's a reason to remember you're not a Cylon, so you better get moving. You better enjoy the things you enjoy, love the people you love, and be kind to people so they'll be kind to you. Isaac Asimov once said, "If my doctor told me I had only six minutes to live, I wouldn't brood. I'd type a little faster." If you started acting like your life had a narrative arc and your job was to develop it, what would you do differently? Would you check Facebook fifty thousand times a day? Care as much whether someone retweets your joke? Spend an hour crafting a snarky reply to a person who is wrong on the Internet? Probably not. You are not a network drama that lasts seventeen seasons longer than it should. You are a human, and humans have beginnings, middles, and ends. So live life more like you're an HBO series. You may have fewer episodes, but you'll have a purpose, and a plot, and you'll leave this world in style. Also you'll curse when it's necessary, because sometimes it is.

The Resilient Fangirl

When it comes to grief and wondering if you'll ever recover, you also have science on your side! Traditionally, psychologists have spent a lot of energy focusing on how humans process grief. The five stages of grief are common knowledge, and we're warned that if we recover too quickly or distract ourselves too much, it'll come back to bite us later on in life. In short, cry now, live later.

George Bonanno, a clinical psychologist at Columbia University, offers a challenge to the traditional understanding of loss. He has studied hundreds of people grieving, and what he has found is quite remarkable. Humans are remarkably resilient creatures, and when we exhibit seemingly abnormal behavior during times of grief, we are actually just doing what we are biologically programmed to do to get by. Say, for example, you forget for a few minutes that your favorite TV show has ended and you laugh at a joke the next day. Or maybe you wonder why you don't cry when your favorite character dies. As humans we are programmed to fluctuate from sadness to joy when we are grieving—if we were in the thick of it all the time, then no one would want to hang around our Debbie Downer selves.

What does this mean for the fangirl? To start, having intense conversations on the Internet or with fangirl friends isn't the complete answer. Bonanno argues that distracting ourselves or avoiding heavy subjects is just as integral a part of the process, and that if we don't take breaks from intensity, we'll be worse off in the long run. When we assume that the grieving process will be long and complicated, it becomes sort of a self-fulfilling prophecy. So the next time you feel the trauma lurking, don't feel ashamed to laugh at YouTube animal compilations or turn your focus onto happier topics. You're a resilient little unicorn, and you'll be just fine.

Endings and Beginnings

A young woman once wrote to me asking whether she should give up on being a fangirl. She explained that whenever she fell in love with a series, she made herself stop before the end. "If I did finish a series, my life would end, and what would I do after that?" she wrote. "It's too intimidating and scary, because when I fangirl over something I can't focus on anything. My grades fall and I can't live in the present. I feel so lonely this way."

Giving your heart to a TV show or a book series is a lot like adopting a dog. You're devoting a lot of time and energy to love something that you will probably outlive (and something that potentially poops on everything you love). So you knowingly hand over your emotions to stories that will end, stories that will leave you sitting on your couch thinking, "Well what do I do with myself now? Rewatch *Buffy*?" Few things are worse than the emotional wasteland that is not having a new show to watch or a new book to read. You know that another will eventually steal your heart, but the waiting is rough.

If you don't think that fictional endings are that powerful, just check the stock market the day after your favorite TV show ends.

British economist Gabriele Lepori looked at 150 major TV series finales between 1967 and 2012, and found that there was a decrease in U.S. stock returns each subsequent day. He assessed that when people are bummed out over the end of a series, there's a decreased demand for assets that are riskier. You don't take chances when you find out your OTP isn't endgame or you're bummed that you'll never see Don Draper again. So whether you're part of a national day-after funk or you've just finished *The West Wing* ten years late, your brain is going to treat the end of a story like any other loss.

Remember how fiction is neurologically transportive? In real life or in fiction, loss can often be just as upsetting as a death.

We lose jobs, fall out of touch with friends, and end relationships. As we age, we slowly lose our mobility, sight, hearing, and memory. We lose family members and friends. I'm not trying to depress you. Humans gain and lose throughout their whole lives. And fangirls especially; how many stories have ended, with the result that you actually thought you couldn't go on? Now you think about them fondly and maybe watch a rerun or reread the book. Why? Because you are resilient. Over time, the fictional loss can become manageable, and you feel grateful for having lived to tell the tale.

But what do you do in the moment or the day after your favorite TV show gets canceled? The loss of a good story strikes a chord in our hearts because the characters were doing something right. It is therefore worth the effort to take some time at the end of a story to reflect. Grab a fangirl friend and talk about what the story meant to you. Don't just reblog gifs, cry on Twitter, and sit there drowning DiCaprio-in-*Titanic* style in your feels. Climb on top of some floating debris and save yourself.

If you're like the reader who could never finish a series, this is my advice to you. I want you to consider that the end of a phenomenal series can be the beginning of something great for you. When I encourage you to take action, I'm not asking you to give up the comfort of cozying up to the imaginary in the first place. I've already talked about how the fangirl world is the stomping ground for testing out your own life narrative. You get to add a pinch of BAMF, turn up the heat in a situation, and see what results. But at some point, everyone's got to step outside the laboratory and start replicating these skills in the broader world. In science, this is what is called generalizability. Which of your fangirl dreams are generalizable to the real world? Maybe you can't turn back time to take two finals at once, but what Hermione Granger–like qualities are worthy of your attention? Latch onto them, and see where they can take you.

The Spin-Off

You hate them, I hate them, everybody hates them. Transitions. They make or break a story. Eventually those *Glee* kids had to graduate from high school. Angel and Addison Montgomery moved to Los Angeles. Someone had to get off that *Lost* island. We are super skeptical when stories change, but nothing is more true to life than the transition chapter. If we didn't have transitions, we'd be like characters in many TV shows— doomed to stay in high school forever or drop out of college and become townies so we can stay in the plot. Like Hannah Horvath on *Girls*, moving across the country to go to grad school suddenly becomes a three-episode arc.

It's no secret that we react to the possibility of change in our own lives like the prospect of a really bad spin-off of our favorite show or remake of our favorite movie. They feel like the evil twin sister to the moments in our lives that felt comfortable and were easy to master. But let me tell you something, friend. You are the lead actor of your own life. You are the only one who can limit yourself to the few parts that you play because the plot will pick itself up and follow you wherever you go. Maybe you're really good at playing the straight-A college student and are considering an indentured servitude of graduate school because it feels like that's all you know how to do. But who's to say that you can't play the fast-talking entrepreneur? The scrappy journalist? The noble teacher? Telling yourself you can't transition into a new phase of life is the equivalent of a casting agent turning down Meryl Streep because she's not right for the role. You don't freaking do it.

Of course there are transitions we don't choose for ourselves. Becoming a motherless daughter was never my choice, but over time I learned that grief gifts in its own way. My first reaction after the initial grief was to yearn for new casting. I kept waiting for some woman to come into my life. A woman who would adopt me and love me as patiently and confidently as my mother had. After a few years of waiting for someone to fill the role, I realized that only I could be that person for myself. That with enough kindness toward myself, enough head pats and good snacks, I would fiercely love the person I am because of, and in spite of, losing my mom. I had thought I was a supporting character in the story of my grief, and I bumped myself up to the main cast.

My life has been full of messy transitions, full of dead ends and plot holes, but I have chosen to keep showing up to see what will happen. I can't guarantee that in your own life there won't be a lot of potentially great spin-offs that will get canceled halfway through the first season. But just like you endured all those horrible sitcoms with your favorite actress, you can get through them until you find a role that sticks. "In the end," Samwise Gamgee reminds us, "it's only a passing thing this shadow. Even darkness must pass. A new day will come, and when the sun shines it'll shine out the clearer." It's hard to know whether you want something to be a part of your story unless you stick around for a few episodes first. So while you're waiting, see what you can glean from fiction. Here are a few exercises to get you started.

VALAR MORGHULIS. Start this exercise by setting a timer for sixty seconds. Write down as many fictional character deaths as you can remember. Whew! Pat yourself on the back for enduring all the juicy pain. Now circle the top three deaths that had the biggest effect on you. Think about one action you can take to honor each of these characters but also build on the narrative of your own life. Maybe you'll volunteer somewhere, or finally take that big risk. You survived your favorite character's death! You are resilient!

PITCH A SPIN-OFF. Pretend you're a screenwriter pitching a TV show spin-off of your life to a powerful executive at a major network. What is the plot, and what motivates your character? What are the challenges you will face as the protagonist? Who are the cast of characters? What is different about this show from the last period of your life? Find a friend who's willing to play the exec and listen to their questions and feedback. This can help you figure out whether your imagined role might be a good transition for your life.

LEGACY LIFTOFF. Often we think of legacies as being the difference we make after we're dead. But any fangirl will tell you that plenty of our faves are living legacies. Take an afternoon or evening and journal about what your vision is for yourself. Who will benefit? What will be the medium in which you achieve the work (an organization, multimedia, writing, etc.)? Finally, decide how much time every day you'd like to dedicate to this work. A life filled with busywork and nothing lasting is, well . . . just busy.

CHAPTER 9
THE FANGIRL RÉSUMÉ

It's 4:19 a.m. and I'm doing a project, but it's all good because I have coffee and Al Green and the imaginary support of Alicia Florrick.

—**CHIARA, EIGHTEEN**

All right kids, I gotta get to work. If I don't input those numbers . . . it doesn't make much of a difference.

—**CHANDLER BING, TRANSPONSTER**

Julianna Margulies's eyebrows changed my life. Yes, it's socially acceptable for a person to say that a self-help book, a religious experience, or a sports team changed their life. But try telling someone a TV show was your turning point, and they'll pat you on the back and point you toward the therapist's office. But the fangirl understands that, more than almost anything, fiction can give us a swift kick in the butt when we're slacking on life. The truth is that show creators Robert and Michelle King's *The Good Wife,* eyebrows and all, is one of the reasons this book exists. One of my graduate students recently called the show "the unsung hero of network TV," and I immediately gave her an A.

When I first watched the complex legal drama, I was in my fifth (!) year of graduate school. Slogging through a doctoral program, I was working as a teaching assistant, a mentor to master's students, a research lackey, and a therapist, all for the sum total of zero dollars and zero cents. So by the summer of 2014, when I stumbled out of my university's basement clinic and into the sunlight, I had paid my dues and then some. All of this free work had somehow resigned me to the conclusion that experience alone was worth the effort. Somehow I had forgotten to advocate for myself. I had no idea how to negotiate a salary or start a business. Colleagues and mentors quipped that the smartest way for a woman to support herself through graduate school was to get married, and they were only half joking.

To quote Liz and Jack from *30 Rock*, "We're not the best, but we're not the worst. Grad students are the worst."

My savior arrived in the form of an unexpected TV binge. In the course of a few weeks, I consumed four and half seasons of *The Good Wife*. Yes, I was in it originally for the hairporn (the hair and power suits on that show are epic), but almost immediately my fangirl senses began to tingle and I sat up and began to take notes. Here were women negotiating their salaries, navigating office politics, and not settling for less than what they deserved. My binge culminated with five words spoken by Christine Baranski's character, Diane Lockhart, that I will never forget: "I want what I'm worth."

My change didn't happen overnight. Inspired by lady BAMFs, I started taking small but shaky steps toward establishing a career as a writer. Because experience alone wasn't going to pay the bills, I started turning down opportunities that weren't compensated. I asked editors who published my essays to start paying me. When strangers emailed me for feedback or advice, I shared my rates with them just like my favorite TV freelancers would. I learned that people would not value me if I did not value my time and efforts first, and that there is no shame in reminding people you can't pay the bills with gratitude. True to my nature, I learned more about my worth from two weeks of fiction than five years of graduate school.

In this chapter I want to teach you how to get what you're worth. I'll share with you some career strategies I've picked up from my own fangirl adventures. We'll talk about how your unicorn skills can make you into a stellar employee, a badass entrepreneur, or whatever you envision for your career. I'll teach you some ninja adulting strategies for when you need to get work done and keep the feels at bay. And finally, you'll learn how to build up immunity to hearing the word *no* so anything can be possible. Let's make that paper, shall we?

Girl's Got Skills

If I could create any job for myself, I would be a Fangirl Guidance Counselor. I'm such a strong advocate for the fangirl because I know in my heart that she makes the best kind of employee. I've been saying this for years on social media while I avoid my work. There is virtually no limit to the number of skills you can put on your résumé thanks to your years of culling every ounce of information from the Internet about your obsessions and from studying fictional human interaction like dedicated anthropologists. In case you don't believe me, here are just a few of the skills that the average fangirl does a thousand times better than the average human.

GOOGLING. No one can hide from us. We can find your email address, your social media accounts, and that embarrassing fanfic that you never wanted to see the light of day. We can encrypt our IP address so you'll never find us. The fangirl can find a pirated video of every play an actress has ever been in and every interview she's ever given. Of course all of these skills can be put to creepy stalker use, but they can also be used for good. "How on earth did you find that email address we needed?" your colleagues ask. "I'm from the Internet," you reply, whipping your cape around as you take off to save their butts yet again.

STAYING CURRENT. The fangirl knows everything that happens the moment it happens. If you want to know which shows are being renewed, when books are coming out, and who's starring in a new pilot, then just ask a fangirl. We are even psychic—or seem to be to those who don't live for spoilers. You want to know what's going to happen three episodes from now on your favorite show? Take a seat and let us tell you.

CRISIS MANAGEMENT. A fangirl is basically a texting hotline for all her friends who are losing their minds over spoilers, plot twists, and character deaths. We can talk ourselves down from a feels spiral and show up to work the next day like the world didn't end (yes, yes it did). If you couldn't think clearly in the midst of chaos, how else would you come up with such hilarious tweets? Writing a great episode recap or movie review requires immediate emotional regulation, and you've got it.

TOTAL DEDICATION. You will ride a sinking ship into the depths of an ocean canyon. You will stick with a show seven seasons after it jumps the shark and becomes awful. Your loyalty rivals Hufflepuff members, and who wouldn't want that quality in a future employee? Social skills and basic time management are overrated when you have *100 percent dedication.*

Still not sure how to translate your fangirl skills into résumé or cover letter text? Let's look at a few examples.

- **FANGIRL:** I have seen every episode of *Supernatural* eight times.

- **TRANSLATION:** I will diligently study new content as long as it takes to achieve understanding and total absorption.

· ·

- **FANGIRL:** I talked my friend down from ALL CAPS texting when *Hannibal* was canceled.

- **TRANSLATION:** I have exceptional crisis management skills and have often been told I am a calming presence in times of uncertainty and transition.

· ·

- **FANGIRL:** I have every paparazzi image of Lupita Nyong'o that has ever existed on my smartphone.

- **TRANSLATION:** I take pride in my organizational and archival skills, which are unrivaled.

· ·

So as you can see, the fangirl is the most dedicated sleuth around. But our Sherlock nature leaves us easily bored when a task isn't as captivating or challenging as our brains demand. So naturally, we get distracted. Our minds wander, our commitment wavers, and suddenly we're clocking in and waiting until we can go home and watch *The 100*. So how do we escape the midseason hiatus–level slog of our lives and jobs?

So Very Distracted

Being a fangirl in today's world is like being a dog off the leash in a squirrel-infested park. We can get what we want whenever we want it, and we're left spinning in circles, barking helplessly at every photo we scroll by on the Internet. When you're like me and you follow fangirls around the world on social media, it's easy to find someone crying about some fictional person every waking second of the day. Our productivity slips out the fire exit as we engage with a diverse, global community of like-minded people. But the highest level of BAMFdom can be achieved only when you harness the power of eliminating distractions.

There's no current clinical diagnosis for Internet addiction, but researchers call it PIU, which stands for problematic Internet use. PIU isn't an illness but it's thought to be a symptom of bigger problems like depression, anxiety, and even suicidal tendencies. In 2015, a Chinese teenager literally chopped off his own hand to make himself stop using the Internet. Fortunately for you, you don't have to go to such extremes to cure your Internet problems. You have me!

PIU can be a huge pothole on your personal road toward adult BAMFdom. About 95 percent of fangirling happens on the Internet, so it's only natural that our habitat gets in the way of a job well done. Multitasking with work while you're G-chatting, texting, and scrolling through Tumblr will actually lower your IQ. Researchers at Carnegie Mellon found that these types of distractions make you approximately 20 percent dumber. And did you know that it takes an average of twenty-five minutes to get refocused on a task after you're interrupted? That means if your best Internet friend is tweeting you pictures of Cate Blanchett every half hour, you are basically screwed.

I know what you're thinking: *If you take away my social media, you are basically taking away my fangirl nature.* Well, it's time to crawl inside the cocoon you've been building and achieve a fanwoman metamorphosis. I'm not perfect, but I have taught myself how to set distractions aside when I need to do so. And I'm here to tell you that there is life and hairporn on the other side, and that fangirling is even sweeter without the guilt of distraction. So if you're ready to start poo-pooing PIU, here are three simple ways to cut back on distractions.

TOMATO TIME! This is a classic work-focus strategy more popularly known as the Pomodoro Technique. Set an alarm for twenty minutes, and then focus on nothing but the task at hand for that time. No texting, no email, no peeing. It is kind of mind-blowing when you begin to realize how much you can get done in a third of an hour. After the alarm sounds, you have five minutes to browse your heart away. Then start again for another cycle. Often I can get most of my boring daily tasks done in two cycles. Or I even find myself wanting to give up my five-minute break and stick with the flow. If you can talk yourself into just one twenty-minute tomato time a day, it will make a huge difference. It's like taking a sledgehammer to Carl and all his nonsense.

SCREENS OFF. One of my goals is to turn off all screens except my phone by 9 P.M. on weekdays. All writing, emailing, Tumblring, and Netflixing has to stop. Yes, I can still tweet people and text friends on my phone, but I try instead to spend that time reading, taking a relaxing shower, or going to bed early. How is this a career skill? Electronics screens are bad for your sleep habits, because the light emitted from them decreases the amount of melatonin in your body and keeps you awake. If you access fewer screens at night, you'll be able to concentrate better on work the next day and have more creative energy. Because of this strategy, I also no longer miss early morning dentist appointments because I stayed up until three in the morning reading *Battlestar Galactica* fanfic on my iPhone.

THE PRIME DIRECTIVE. Just like *Star Trek*'s United Federation of Planets had a guiding principle, you need one for your workday as well. If you don't, you won't jeopardize civilizations but you will endanger your productivity. There is a difference between being effective and being efficient. Between what is important and what is urgent. If I spend my day answering emails, decluttering my workspace, and organizing my desktop folders, have I really accomplished anything? So every morning I ask myself: What is my prime directive for today? If I could accomplish only one thing, what would it be? Then I finish that one task before I do anything else. Because I often work from home, sometimes I don't even let myself shower before I finish it. For me, this task is usually writing a thousand words. And after those words exist, no matter how badly written they are, I'm allowed to go about my day. Finishing your directive will make you feel more productive and less anxious. You'll be more focused and fret less, and you won't feel guilty if you do spend some time wading through TMZ or those drama queen Tumblrs you always creep on. In short, you'll live long and prosper.

Please Reject Me

So we know that you've got the skill, but have you got the stomach? Professional success and extreme adulting mean being able to hear the word *no* and not holing up in your feels bunker. The most marketable skill isn't a trade or specialized knowledge, it's the ability to be rejected over and over and still stand up and show up. A few years ago, I decided to go on a failure crusade. It all started when I sent a story idea to a big newspaper, asking them if I could write about my work with therapy clients. They liked the idea, and I sent them the first draft, which was returned with encouraging feedback. I edited and sent in a second draft. And then I never heard from them again, despite many emails.

Eventually, however, I decided that changing the narrative was more effective than huffing and puffing down to the newspaper's headquarters. I couldn't control their reactions, but I could edit my own story and try harder. This wasn't a story about me getting rejected from a newspaper. It was a story of me getting better and better at hearing no and surviving. About developing an immunity that would serve me well in my career. My new mission was to get rejected every day by at least one publication. Sure it didn't feel amazing, but I kept my cool over rejection emails and started composing new pitches. I thanked my rejecters for their quick responses rather than being a snarky crybaby. In a way, I had chosen to jump the shark on my own life. I was taking chances and trying something new, and I couldn't care less what the critics said.

This book exists because I flipped my laptop open after a long day at work and took the time to try to get rejected by a literary agency. A few days later I was on the bus, stuck in traffic. As I checked my email, my eyes grew anime-size. I jerked the cord for the next stop and exploded out of the bus. I sprinted down the street screeching like a rabid giraffe. In my great rejection quest, I had gotten a yes—all because I had taught myself not to be afraid of a no.

What I want you to understand from this story is that the only no that can really do damage is the one that you give yourself. When you listen to Carl and don't take the chance to do something brave, you're risking more than when you throw an idea out or apply for that promotion. A no or yes doesn't separate conquering fangirls from the ones who stay stuck. It's the willingness to get that rejection and keep going. There are endless real people stories of those who heard no and kept going. Oprah was told she wasn't right for television. Lucille Ball was told she was too shy to be an actress. Madonna was working at Dunkin' Donuts in Times Square. Nobody noticed Jon Hamm or Harrison Ford for many years. *Harry Potter and the Philosopher's Stone* was rejected by publishers twelve times! The lesson here isn't that people are idiots. It's that rejection is part of the story, but it doesn't have to be the end of it. Let's look at some fictional characters who didn't exactly succeed at their initial professional endeavors.

- Tom Haverford (*Parks and Rec*) created multiple businesses that failed

- George O'Malley (*Grey's Anatomy*) screwed up his first surgery

- Peggy Olson (*Mad Men*) was refused a raise

- Tami Taylor (*Friday Night Lights*) lost her job as a principal

- Harry Potter couldn't pull off a Patronus Charm

There are many more examples in fiction, but as we discussed earlier, more often than not, protagonists get what they want. Real life is so much harder! But as a fangirl, you put yourself out there all the time. You are the Han Solo of the Internet, shouting "Never tell me the odds!" as you add your voice to the mix. How many tweenage girls tweet Harry Styles every single second, hoping he might reply to them? It looks like he gets an average of 180 tweets a minute. There are 1,400 minutes in a day, so that's 259,200 tweets. It looks like he replies to people about once a week. So that means your odds of getting a reply are 1 in 1,814,400, which is lower than your odds of buying a single ticket and winning millions of dollars in the Powerball lottery.

But you still do it anyway, don't you? You thank actors and artists because (1) you appreciate them and (2) you want them to know it. You might look a little foolish, but the cost is worth it. So why aren't you willing to look a little foolish in front of people you've never even met, like editors and job recruiters, and without broadcasting it to the entire Internet? We tend to underestimate how easy it is to get in contact with powerful people who aren't celebrities, aka the people who can get us where we want to go. But the truth is that an email or a phone call or an invitation to coffee can literally change your life. Gumption is what truly separates the successful from the timid.

Just Say Nah

The flip side to jumping for opportunities is knowing when to say no to dead-ends and distractions. I am somewhat of a professional quitter. When things don't work for me, I bid farewell without a tear. I've lived in seven different cities since college, and I've had seventeen jobs in the last ten years, from teaching eighth-grade boys *Romeo and Juliet* to developing phone apps for people with diabetes. And we can't forget that one job where I got paid to read *People* magazine to Korean immigrants. That was the best one.

I didn't quit these jobs because I was a bad employee. And I didn't move because I hated those cities. I was just floating downstream, finding what was right for me. At first Carl was hella harsh because he thought I needed to have my entire life planned. But now I see that my twenties were the time to make the mistakes. Date the wrong people. Maybe even get the graduate degree I'd never use. My nightmare wasn't unemployment or spinsterdom. It was getting stuck and staying stuck in the wrong job or relationships. Waking up at fifty and never having taken any chances. I didn't want the fear of failure to snuff out dreams again and again.

Fangirls can be 100 percent dedicated, but we can also say nah to a show or a book that just isn't doing it for us. So you should be able to do the same for your own life. Now that doesn't mean I want you to leave your job the second it gets rough. There are lots of ways to practice eliminating the unnecessary from your daily life. Sometimes creating a not-to-do list can be even more effective than creating a to-do list. Build up your nah-saying ability with these tasks.

- Stopping a book if it sucks
- Quitting a TV show when it's jumped the shark
- Blocking websites that distract you
- Unsubscribing from emails that are irrelevant
- Saying no to social obligations that provide no joy
- Not texting people back when they're stirring up drama

Once you've built up your no muscle, it can become easier to start hatching a new plot for your career and your life. Comfort will lose its appeal when you catch a glimpse of what's over the next hill.

A Season of Purpose

If you're wondering why I haven't made any career suggestions for fangirls in this chapter, it's because you can be *anything*. Professional hair petter, romance novelist, bounty hunter, president—you name it, and you can be it. Think of how enormous your passion is for your tiniest fictional headcanon, and then imagine how far your dedication to a real endeavor could go. So before I send you on your way, let me tuck just a few bits of reality into your fangirl briefcase.

FICTIONAL JOBS ARE NOT REAL LIFE JOBS. Don't become a surgeon because you think you'll get to have a lot of sex in the break room like a *Grey's Anatomy* character. If you watched a lot of *CSI* over the years, perhaps you've forgotten that crime scene investigators usually don't fly around in helicopters. Professors aren't flipping their chairs backward to give impromptu library lectures in tweeds. Vampire slayers (probably) don't exist. Fiction can be a great starting point for brainstorming career ideas, but you've got to throw yourself into a real-world environment to see if you like it. Ask someone who's in a profession that interests you if you can shadow her for a day, and then decide whether you can see yourself cast in that kind of role.

TWENTY-TWO IS NOT A MAGIC AGE. There are people who decide their career path when they are twelve, and then there are those of us who want to do anything and everything. And that's okay! What's key is getting up every morning and asking yourself, "What is the most important thing I can do today?" Because often the answer to that question will be to scratch that itch, to test the waters of a dream you have. Maybe you will fail oh so spectacularly. Maybe you'll succeed. Maybe you'll decide something isn't meant for you. Regardless, you won't wake up and be sixty-two and wonder, What if? There's a difference between pursuing something and committing to it for forty years.

OTHER WOMEN WILL SUCCEED. If you're keeping the right company, then you'll have surrounded yourself with women who want to conquer just as much as you do. TV and movies love to trick us into thinking that two women wanting the same thing are destined enemies. But the faster you learn to stop competing with other women, the sooner you'll realize that keeping them in your camp is the best thing that could have happened to you. The only real competition is between you and Carl. And Carl is winning if he can distract you into believing that ugly media trope: you get less when another fangirl gets more. Science tells us that happy people are able to celebrate others' successes. It's not a talent that you have or don't have—it's a muscle you have to flex every day to remind yourself you're not the center of the universe. Which leads us to the next principle.

YOU ARE NOT THE CENTER OF THE UNIVERSE. When you're mapping out your goals, it's easy to become hyperfocused on issues like status and money. But I'm going to guess that all your favorite fictional folks shine brightest when they turn the focus outward and real life is no different. A life with purpose is also a life of service. What that service will look like is up to you. Whatever you choose, it should be your weekly and even daily reminder that not everything is about you. The best shows happen when characters share screen time. Don't be that diva who thinks the camera loves her more than anyone else. Shine the light on a story that's worth telling and the people who can tell it.

On your journey to BAMFdom, you may have to keep the same boring day job to pay the rent for a while, but that doesn't mean you can't summon your fangirl powers to start taking a few brave steps toward something great. And remember, just as your fangirl passions are constantly changing, your hopes and dreams shouldn't be any different. I don't know what I want to be when I grow up, but I'm having the best time figuring it out. As the fangirls say, be the Leslie Knope of whatever you do, and live a life full of heart and epic mistakes and inspiring ladies. Jump at opportunities whenever they arise, and don't stop to doubt yourself. Ignore Carl the Weatherman who's forever forecasting your doom. Here are some ideas to get your feet moving.

BAMF COFFEE HOUR. Just like fangirling is a team effort, your career strategizing shouldn't be a solo activity. We all enjoy seeing our friends, we like cackling as we plot to take over the world, and coffee is yum. So why not combine all

three? Create a Facebook invite for a BAMF Coffee Hour and invite your squad for an hour of career talk. If people live far away, organize a virtual meeting. My fangirl friends and I used to host a Thursday night online meeting where we'd each commit to one BAMFy action for the week. Encourage each other to take risks and ask for that salary bump you deserve. You'll have a wonderful time sharing and scheming.

CAREER LADY PLAYLIST. We can all name those favorite episodes where our girl crush hands everyone their collective butts, whether in a courtroom, a classroom, or a shootout. But instead of watching them late at night while you're shoving hummus in your face, why not watch a quick clip before work or a big meeting? Use their powers to your advantage, and psych yourself up to conquer. Practice a power pose while you watch, and feel the confidence flow through you.

CHAPTER 10
FANWOMAN

I love women who have been through hell and back and sort of say, "screw you" to their situation and rise above it. Women who are flawed and learn to embrace their flaws and use them to their advantage. Women who don't need men to survive. Women who don't need to put down other women to survive.

—DEBORAH, TWENTY-TWO

I am big enough to admit I am often inspired by myself.

—LESLIE KNOPE, *PARKS AND RECREATION*

Here at last, on the shores of BAMF Island, we have come to the end of our fangirl fellowship. There were plenty of chances for you to turn back, but you didn't because you believe that there is good in fangirling, and it's worth fighting for. But maybe, just maybe, you have some doubts about this whole conquering thing. A few years ago a fangirl wrote to me asking whether she had what it took to be like the women she admired in real life and in fiction. "I don't think I deserve to be like that. I don't think that I have such great qualities in me, such morals and courage," she wrote. "Is this possibly true?" This last chapter is for her, and for all the fangirls who wonder the very same thing.

For our last few pages, I'm going to psych you up to live like a champion, and I'll provide you with a few hints about the obstacles that might impede your journey to fanwoman. But like any expedition, you'll need some company to keep you entertained and motivated. So first let's talk about the most important ship you will ever board. Our work is almost finished, and you must choose the company you will keep as you move forward. (I may not have been to Mordor and back, but I've driven to Cleveland at 3 A.M. with a fangirl friend, and that's pretty much the same thing. Trudging on through the darkness in her mom's minivan, we were on a mission to watch a *Downton Abbey* season premiere with our Internet friends.)

You're never going to be able to live the fanwoman life if

you don't have friends along for the journey. Despite every fictional pairing that has stolen my heart, friendship is the greatest ship that fangirling has given me. Though we may range in age, culture, and geography, there is this unicorn bond that forms when someone has seen you at your absolute craziest. When you have spent hours discussing hairporn or wading through your many concerns about your fic update. We interact with one another without shame or inhibition, like children or the best improv players, and we're not discussing real estate prices, or mutual funds, or whether Bill Pullman or Bill Paxton starred in *Independence Day*. We're creating stories.

There is a force in the universe that is stronger than sharing most common hobbies or interests like sports or knitting, and that force is the choice to invest in the same story, no matter the outcome. Fangirl friends travel with us through the dark forests of love triangles, the valleys of hiatus, or the caves full of horrible fandom trolls. When you think about it, that's a lot like "till death do us part." You can limit your fangirl friendship to that commitment to fiction, which in itself is wonderful. Or you can take that bond a step further into everyday life, and make the commitment to invest in each other's stories. To promise to be present during those boring filler episodes of life and during the worst sweeps weeks when the unthinkable occurs. To listen to each other's hopes with as much interest as you give the best headcanon. It's a lonely road if you aren't willing to find other women willing to join you. So think about who you want by your side when you set out into uncharted territory.

Clear Eyes, Full Hearts, Can BAMF

I don't like to think of this chapter as the end of our time together. You'll find my disembodied presence floating around on
Twitter or Tumblr, and we'll keep crying about hairporn. If it
helps, think of the end of this book as more of a halftime break.
We're all huddled in the locker room, sweaty and huffing from
a difficult first half. There have been a couple of setbacks, distractions from the Internet or real-life responsibilities. We lost
a couple of readers back in the early chapters, so our numbers

have dwindled. You can hear the faint roar of the restless crowd as I knock my stool out of the way and I kneel down in front of you. Knowing me, I'd probably start mashing together quotes from *Friday Night Lights* in my authentic southern accent.

But instead of speechifying, let's focus on a basic truth: No single success or failure will be what defines your role in life. Good character development happens when you show up every day and be kind to others and yourself. When you are willing to take risks and see what could happen when you open yourself to the possibility of a new chapter of life. So before you close this book, I'd like you to do one last exercise with me. Go grab a pen and some paper, and meet me back here.

I want you to draw a big circle. Good job. Now inside the big circle, I want you to draw a smaller one. Four for you, Glen Coco! Now label the big circle OOC. If you're in fandom, you know that this acronym stands for "out of character." This typically refers to an actor stepping out of her role-play character to talk, but in fan fiction the term can describe an action that does not ring true for a character. Finally, label the smaller, inner circle IC (for "in character"). Using the circles, I want you to jot down and organize all the decisions you make in a day or a week. For instance:

OOC Decisions

- Going along with the group

- Putting down others to feel good

- Needing to be liked by everyone

- Holding or conforming to stereotypes

IC Decisions

- Standing up for my beliefs

- Using facts instead of emotions

- Following my passions

- Being true to myself

As a fangirl, you are really good at pointing out when fic writers or screenwriters make one of your favorite fictional folks do something that is OOC (like season 6 sad Lorelai Gilmore). But how good are you at identifying those moments and decisions in your own life? If you're living a life of character development, you are working to grow that inner circle. Yes, you will get ragey sometimes or feel the need to blend in with the group. But the more your decisions can represent your authentic self, the less you are guided by the whims of feels and anxieties, and the more you become a character worth rooting for. This kind of inside-out living is never easy and never quick. But if you show up every day and run the lines again and again, eventually you'll strengthen the muscles you need to develop your character. To make the bold moves you've been waiting for since season 1.

The Hurdles Ahead

Making bold moves in real life is always harder than it is in fiction. Every character you admire gets a thousand restarts in life. You make up new headcanon, write fics, and rewatch a season a million times, filling in the blanks as you please. But you don't get an alternate universe life. You get one story, one chance to embody and pursue the directions your interests take you. Think about what tomorrow would be like if you wrote yourself a fresh script. What would be different? What lines would you write for yourself? What plot bunnies would you chase down and wrangle? What meaning would you derive from the twists and turns of the unexpected? In this book I shared many strategies for making bold moves in life, but following a clear strategy also means being aware of the challenges that can stand in your way. Here are three hurdles you're likely to meet on your fangirl journey.

THE WHISPERS. Regardless of whether you give them a name or not, there will always be voices living inside your head. The Carls who will tell you that you will never be like the people you admire in fiction. They'll whisper that you are not smart enough, beautiful enough, or anything enough. *Enough* is the worst word there ever was. Be aware that the more you push yourself toward the uncomfortable, the louder and more insistent these voices may become. But listen closely, and you'll find that there are other voices living inside your head. They are the voices of your favorite Broadway actress when you were a child, or your favorite Hogwarts instructor. That one superhero or TV lawyer who always did what was right when no one else stood up. That one BAMFy lady who is prepared to end everyone who gets in her way. You carry these voices because at one point or another, they spoke to the part of you that lies tucked away behind your insecurities. They can't be explained by science, but what's wrong with a little magic? As the great Fox Mulder once asked, "When convention and science offer us no answers, might we not finally turn to the fantastic as a plausibility?" And you, my friend, are one fantastic fanwoman.

THE SAFE NARRATIVE. What will this transformation look like for you? You probably won't wake up tomorrow with perfect one-liners and hair styled with unicorn tears. You might still feel the pressure to fit in or make sure that everyone is happy with you and your choices. You'll feel the pull of the safe narratives that this world offers you, the temptation to fall in step, to not rock the boat, and to not make too many animal noises when you watch TV. You'll still feel the need to nestle your psyche into fanfic when things get tense, and a nap will always seem like a better option than asking for what you're worth. I give you permission to be that way right now. But on top of that layer of security blanket actions, there should be bold moves sprinkled here and there. You'll start to test the daring narrative that isn't handed to you by the world. You may not be as confident as Emma Thompson when your professor asks for your opinion when you disagree with him, but you can be strong when your pizza has the wrong toppings and the delivery man is refusing to fix the situation. Look for small but significant ways to start nudging yourself in the direction of the fanwoman.

THE LONE TRAVELER.

Your other temptation will be to convince yourself that you are the last unicorn. But the more amazing women you have in your life, the more you empower yourself to live a truly amazing narrative. Every day can be Galentine's Day if you want it to be. Surround yourself with positive people who know their passions, who don't apologize for their decisions, and who don't humor the haters. Don't hesitate to find these ladies in your own fandom. Take the occasional break from headcanon talk to dare each other to be great. Don't be afraid to tell a social media fandom acquaintance you would like to get to know her. Everyone loves admirers, and a true BAMF will want to pay it forward to the next generation. Your BAMF network should also consist of fangirl friends who can hold you accountable for taking risks and honoring the character traits of the people you admire in fiction. Energy and inspiration are contagious when you report your successes and your struggles.

So Long, Farewell

My hope for you is that years from now, when you look back, you'll be proud of how your character unfolded. That when you're seventy and floating through virtual reality TV shows, smelling actresses' hair, and choosing your own adventure, you'll look back on the past seasons of your life and say you lived one hell of a story. Deep down you'll know that no new fiction, no matter how innovative, can take the place of the first shows and books that inspired you to live your life like it mattered. Tucked in your heart will remain those characters who encouraged you to be your authentic self regardless of who was watching.

As you've read this book, perhaps you've collected some Easter eggs of advice and insights that can prove relevant to you on your fangirl journey. Or maybe you've already reached a respectable level of maturity in your day-to-day life. But most of us, regardless of our age, can get developmentally stuck when it comes to our unicorn nature. We're not fangirls, but we're not really fanwomen either. Is fanwoman an oxymoron? Do we cease to be fan-anythings the second we become able to appreciate an actor in a mature manner? No! I believe in my heart of hearts that there is a whole generation of fanwomen waiting to unleash our BAMFiness all over the land. Because being a fanwoman was never about shaking off your fictional passions. It's about finally being able to take those passions and plug them into your life story.

Soon you'll return to the field of life, and you can make the excuses: that the book wasn't for you, or that there are fangirls worse than you. And you can revert to the status quo, to letting anxiety keep you from moving outside your comfort zone. You know that fate has bestowed you with supernatural senses. You see grace in the goofy and hope in the horrible. You have the ability to stop and smell the awesome, but can you grab it? Because that is what separates the fangirls from the fanwomen. So don't let the first draft of yourself be the final draft. We dive into stories of true courage, but they compel us because they are full of unfinished people. Yes, your favorite characters might stick to their morals and seem fearless, but they can be extraordinarily horrible like the rest of us. They're flawed creatures who manage to rise up and embrace their humanity more often than not.

As a fangirl, you are an anxious creature, a curious creature, and sometimes a discouraged one. But you are not a finished one. And your own story is worth sticking with to see what could happen. You don't watch the credits of *The Empire Strikes Back,* turn to your dog, and go, "That was a nice story. Let's see what's on Bravo." You plow forward and hit play on *Return of the Jedi* because there's no way Han Solo can just stay trapped in carbonite forever.

That is the point where we find ourselves now. We can change the channel and never find out how hot Harrison Ford was in 1983. Or we can show up and finish the job that we started the day that first badass lady waltzed into our imaginations. The day your mouth flopped open from the wonder of a new fictional world. Because I am not finished with myself, and neither are you.

So go. Climb every mountain. Ford every stream. You can't stay all your life down at the heel, looking out of the window, staying out of the sun. Somewhere beyond the barricade is there a world you long to see? If you're on fire, show me! And while you're at it, do all the other Broadway lyrics that sound inspiring too. Do whatever it takes to make yourself get excited about your own story. But also remember that any fictional story that makes you squee is not a toy you have to retire to the attic. Those stories are your weapons to keep the haters at bay. Those ships are your fuel to love and be loved. And those characters are your confidantes and consultants as you negotiate your dreams with the rest of the world. They have made you the person you are today, and they will still be there when the next season of your life begins. And let's be honest. What's more exciting than a brand new season? The script is yours, and you're the star. So give us something worth watching.

FANGIRL DICTIONARY

ANGST—canon storyline or fan fiction that is dark and depressing, often in which characters suffer from not being able to be together or unrequited love.

ATTHS—and then they have sex. Can be used when a fic writer does not want to write an explicit sex scene.

AU—alternate universe. Type of fan fiction that puts characters into different worlds, genres, time periods, or scenarios outside of canon.

BAMF—badass mother effer. Among fangirls it often refers to a strong, independent female character.

BAMFSFERENCE—portmanteau of *BAMF* and transference. Occurs when a fangirl is attracted to a lady BAMF's love interest simply because they worship and respect her.

BETA—a person who edits and proofreads fan fiction.

BROTP—play on the acronym OTP, referring to a fangirl's favorite two characters who are (or should be in your humble opinion) best friends.

Fangirl Dictionary

CANON—the official storyline established by the author, show creator, or the like. When a ship is referred to as canon, it is real in the show, book, or movie.

COSPLAY—costume play. When fans dress up to portray fictional characters.

CRACKSHIP—an appealing romantic pairing that is unlikely to happen in canon.

CREYS—a more intense form of feels that usually follows a negative development in plot. *My crey* is the phrase often uttered.

CROSSOVER—a fanfic where characters from different TV shows, books, and so on interact. It can also refer to an episode of a TV show where characters from different shows interact.

DONE—used by the fangirl when something excites her or causes an intense emotional reaction, positive or negative.

ENDGAME—when a fictional pairing is together at the end of a book or series.

FANDOM—the community formed by fans.

FAN FICTION—story written by a person who did not create the original character or plot.

FANGIRL—a lady fan.

FANVID—a fan-made video consisting of clips accompanied by music.

FEELS—fangirl word for feelings. Refers to intense wave of emotion that is desirable and often unavoidable.

FIC—fan fiction (abbreviation).

FLUFF—type of fan fiction that is typically happy, is often G rated, and involves shameless flirting between characters and little to no plot.

FOETP—two fictional people who make the perfect nemeses.

GIF—computer image that moves as animation. Gifs are used by fangirls in lieu of words to express their emotions and reactions. Some debate over whether it is pronounced with a hard or soft g sound. (It's a hard *G*.)

GPOY—gratuitous picture of yourself. Often used when a fangirl relates on some level to an image.

HAIRPORN—really, really, really pretty hair as captured on film.

HBIC—head bitch in charge.

HEADCANON—additional information/narrative about a character that is not canon but is accepted as true by the fangirl, a group of fangirls, or an entire fandom.

HIATUS—period of time when TV show is on break.

I CAN'T—uttered by fangirl when she is overcome with emotion. Usually interchangeable with the word *done*.

I HATE YOUR FACE—uttered by fangirl when an actor/actress is ridiculously attractive.

JUMP THE SHARK—used to describe when a show begins to decline in quality because writers use desperate gimmicks to get viewers' attention. Originates from a scene in *Happy Days* when Fonzie jumps over a shark on water skis.

LADYGOGGLES—metaphorical eye gear for watching a TV show strictly for the female characters.

LIFE-RUINER—someone who is so unbelievably perfect that it ruins your life in the best way. Ugh.

MAL—middle-aged lady.

MANIP—photo manipulation; often made by crackshippers to show two characters kissing.

META—nonfiction writing that explores themes, character development, and other facets of a fictional work.

NOTP—opposite of OTP. A fangirl's least favorite pairing.

OOC—out of character. Used in role-playing when a person wants to step outside of character or when a fangirl describes a character's actions as not authentic to the original character.

OFB—outrageously fancy behavior.

OTP—one true pairing. The OTP is the fangirl's favorite fictional romantic relationship and often the one that causes the most pain and suffering.

RPG—role-playing game. When a person takes on the persona of a fictional character. RPGs can be played in person or online.

SHIP—n. relationship (abbreviation). v. to want two characters to be involved in a romantic relationship.

SLASH—fan fiction that involves two male characters in a relationship.

SLAY—to conquer and do something totally amazing.

SMUT—fan fiction that is erotic in nature.

SORKINING—fast-paced sanctimonious speechifying with a liberal bent. Can be Ambulatory Sorkining (brisk walking down office hallways) or Stationary.

SQUEE—portmanteau of the words *squeal* and *glee*. Natural onomatopoetic noise released from the fangirl when she is excited.

SQUEEFLAIL—when a fangirl produces the squee sound while implying moving her body in excitement, usually imitating a bird flapping its wings.

STAN—portmanteau of *stalker* and *fan*. Also sometimes refers to a fan who is less concerned with ships and more focused on the celebrity/character as an individual.

SWEEPS WEEK—periods when rates for TV ads are set based on the number of viewers. Originated when the Nielson Company sent TV Diaries to households and asked them to record their TV viewing habits. Usually something dramatic or shark-jumping happens on shows to increase viewership. This method is a dying practice, however, with many shows no longer on traditional networks and fewer seasons running on the fall to spring schedule.

TGTGT—totally gratuitous totally gay touching.

TRASH—joking term used by fangirl to describe herself when she is powerlessly fixated on a particular show or ship.

TROLL—Internet meanie intent on causing arguments and chaos.

UNICORN—used to describe someone who is unique.

WHAT IS AIR?—question asked by the fangirl when she is unable to breathe from laughing so hard.

ENGLISH TO FANGIRL PHRASE BOOK

Fangirl is a fairly easy language to pick up. Dictionaries can help, but like any language, you have to toss yourself into a foreign country and learn from the native speakers. Here are a few practice phrases to get you started.

- **ENGLISH:** That was a very touching moment.

- **FANGIRL:** CRYING. So done. *flies into the sun*

. . . .

- **ENGLISH:** She is very attractive in that photograph.

- **FANGIRL:** I hate your face.

. . . .

- **ENGLISH:** I think they would make a nice couple.

- **FANGIRL:** And then there's these two idiots.

· ·

- **ENGLISH:** That scene was particularly sad.

- **FANGIRL:** Drowning in feels. My crey.

· ·

- **ENGLISH:** I can't rewatch that scene. It's too painful.

- **FANGIRL:** How about a giant bowl of NOPE.

· ·

- **ENGLISH:** Please do not mention that to me.

- **FANGIRL:** WHO GAVE YOU THE RIGHT.

· ·

- **ENGLISH:** I really like this.

- **FANGIRL:** I can't even. I've lost the ability to can.

· ·

- **ENGLISH:** This initiates an intense emotional reaction in me.

- **FANGIRL:** All the feels.

· ·

- **ENGLISH:** This is my favorite character.

- **FANGIRL:** Actual best.

. . . .

ACKNOWLEDGMENTS

Many amazing people contributed their wisdom to this book. Thanks to editor Jeanette Shaw for turning rambles into truths, agent Hannah Brown Gordon for believing in an email from a fangirl, and artist Camilla Fiocchi for your brilliance and enthusiasm. Thanks to the ridiculously wonderful Jacob Heim for humoring me and cheering me on the entire way. Also, many hugs to the fangirl committee, Ame Roberts, Lauren Bray, and Rachel Wall, my heroes and future BAMF Camp counselors. I'm indebted to all the beautiful online and offline friends who shared their stories and feels with me. My life is better with you in it, and I hope to get to meet every single one of you someday. Finally, thank you fictional people who live in my brain. I will never ever evict you, and I promise to listen more closely to what you can teach me.

ABOUT THE AUTHOR

KATHLEEN SMITH is a licensed professional counselor and mental health journalist who lives in Washington, D.C. She is the creator of the blog FangirlTherapy.com, where she answers questions about the fangirl brain. In her free time, she searches for middle-aged OTPs and good friends who cry about them.